Andi Thomas &
Alexander Netherton

Are You An Ostrich?

A Diary of the 2014/15 Premier League

www.ockleybooks.co.uk

Ockley Books Ltd

www.ockleybooks.co.uk

First published 2015

ISBN 978-1910906019

Front Cover, layout and illustrations by Michael Kinlan

Premier League shirt illustrations by www.mehibi.com

Printed & bound in Scotland by:

Bell & Bain, Glasgow,

www.bell-bain.com

“

I HAVE SEEN A LADY WHO PLAYS THE SAXOPHONE FANTASTICALLY. GIVE HER BIG APPLAUSE.

“

Louis van Gaal

CONTENTS

CONTENTS

FOREWORD

By Des Kelly

WHENEVER I am looking for something interesting to read I head straight to my nearest bookshop and lift a thick, magnificently-bound diary from the shelf.

That gives me something to stand on while I reach for a proper book.

I can say without any fear of contradiction that, as far as I'm concerned, the book in your hands ranks alongside some of the most important diaries ever written, be it by Anne Frank, Samuel Pepys or Adrian Mole.

Because I haven't read those either.

The idea someone would be so self-obsessed to routinely scribble down their inane, innermost thoughts at the end of the day is faintly repellent. It's nothing more than a literary selfie.

The majority of the diaries also happen to be whiney and boring, played in out in some imaginary universe where some dull diary writer imagines they are dead centre of everything.

If that's what you want from a diary, then put this work back immediately and look up Alastair Campbell.

But if you want humour and an entertainingly loose relationship with actual events (something the authors may share with the aforementioned Campbell) then you have choice.

You can opt for The Hitler diaries, flick through Bridget Jones or enjoy... er, what's it called again? Hang on, it's here somewhere. Ah, yes. "Are You An Ostrich?"

The unforgettable title obviously relates to Nigel Pearson's notoriously bizarre press conference rant where he tried to belittle a journalist for daring to ask a question. Afterwards, I'm told the reporter was ostrich-sized.

(Oh come on. Read it again. That joke is as good as any you're likely to find in this book.)

Luckily, I am assured by the people who read these kind of manuscripts for me that there are more than enough topically humorous remarks included in these chapters.

I'm also told there is also an excerpt where Jose Mourinho describes how he would like to urinate from the balcony of his office onto the "ant-like minions below".

On reflection, that anecdote may be from the diary of former Conservative Minister Alan Clark, which means I have mixed up my notes.

I'm afraid you'll have to read this book to find out if that's the case. I hope to do so myself any day now. I'll make a note in my diary.

Des Kelly is a presenter on BT Sport, a TalkSPORT host and columnist for The London Evening Standard.

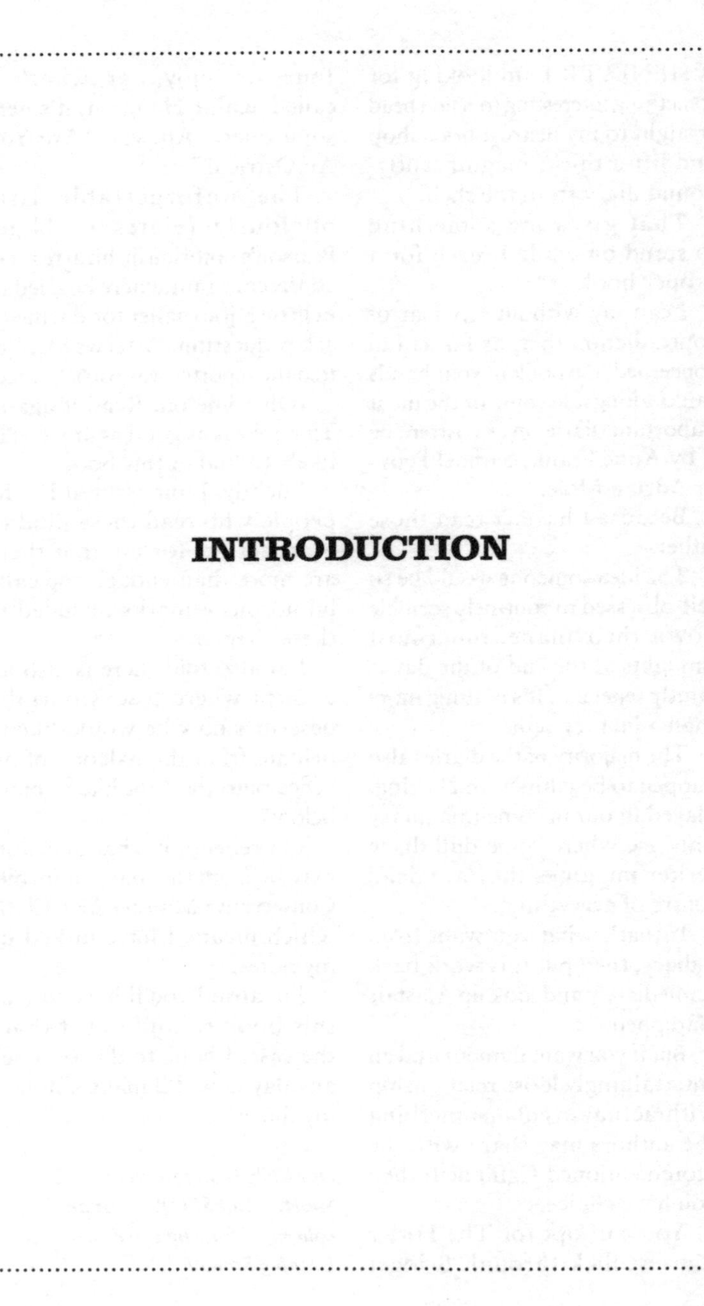

INTRODUCTION

Welcome to another year of the Diary[1].

If you are one of the few people who are reading it for the third successive season, hello to our mums and dads. If you are someone who is trying it for the first time, then I don't care, Ian, you'll never be anything more than a step-dad and pretending to be interested in my work isn't going to make me like you.

The season has been, as the Chinese teacher Consensus decided, a boring one. This is because Chelsea won, and from the first few weekends it was always apparent that Chelsea would win the league. That's boring if you watch football purely from the perspective on the football alone, and even then Chelsea were far more entertaining than people credit them for.

For the opening half of the season Chelsea obliterated teams with their organisation, pace, and ruthlessness. It was exciting football, it's just that they were so good at it that the novelty wore off quickly, and the disappointment should not be with the season or Chelsea's slip-off in the second half. It should be with Manchester City, Arsenal, Manchester United and Liverpool, who allowed them such an easy way to the title despite the wobble in the stodgy part of the season.

But that doesn't take into account most of the rest of the season. If you're solely interested in the results, goals, tackles and the league table, that's up to you, but there's so much more of the season to be considered before you can properly call it boring.

You have Louis van Gaal bowling around the league with a near-constant setting of belligerence to all in front, next to and behind him, making it up as he goes along and slapping Ryan Giggs in the face, all occasionally interrupted by some obviously sincere moments of being a pleasant man, such as toasting journalists at Christmas or celebrating his end of season party with a berserker performance.

You have Brendan Rodgers, never knowingly not worth a joke at his expense as he buries himself under hubristic bullshit. You have Arsenal fans celebrating another year of winning the Calendar Year Title[2]. You have Jose Mourinho flicking Vs and rekindling grand conspiracies. You have Manchester City, a charisma void of a club, doing PR for oil and gas money with a mixture of Innocent Smoothie Corporatespeak and vast wealth. And lastly, you have Nigel Pearson, ruddy-faced, telling a journalist, "I think you are an ostrich."

1 And another year of the footnotes!

2 You'd think it would be mathematically impossible to be the best team over 12 months and not pick up a title or two. But you'd be wrong.

If you're looking at the pitch and turning your nose up, you may have a point. If you're experiencing the season as a whole and deciding that it's boring, then Stuart Pearce, please stop reading now.

We'd like to say thank you to Ed Malyon and Jack Lang, and all those at the Mirror who edited the columns most weeks and published them on the site. Also, to Nick Miller, Matt Stanger, Sarah Winterburn and Daniel Storey for their help in doing the same for the 2013/14 diary on Football 365. To Richard Whittall, for running the very first year's diary on The Score. To the handsome Des Kelly, who wrote the foreword despite receiving substantially less than his usual £10 a word fee. And lastly to all the people who tweeted us each week, 'Did it really take two people to write this?' Yes. It did.

AUGUST 16th

Arsenal 2-1 Crystal Palace
Leicester 2-2 Everton
Manchester United 1-2 Swansea
QPR 0-1 Hull
Stoke 0-1 Aston Villa
West Bromwich 2-2 Sunderland
West Ham 0-1 Tottenham

AUGUST 17th

Liverpool 2-1 Southampton
Newcastle 0-2 Manchester City

AUGUST 18th

Burnley 1-3 Chelsea

In keeping with its reputation for Pulitzer-winning investigative journalism, the Diary had exclusive access to the talks between managers and their chief executives as they planned for the season ahead. What follows is a not-at-all-fictional set of conversations that could shock football to its core. Its shiny, Gazprom-drenched core.

ARSENE WENGER AND IVAN GAZIDIS[1]

Wenger: "I want Alexis Sanchez to link up with Debuchy on the right wing. Crystal Palace shouldn't provide much opposition. The most important thing is that we don't let up this year. Last time we struggled with a slight lack of quality and strength in depth.

"Calum Chambers will be alongside Laurent Koscielny, so he's going to be the senior partner at the start of the season. Per Mertesacker will be phased in over the first few weeks as he rests from the World Cup, but this is a great chance for Chambers to learn, and he's also adept at right-back should Debuchy struggle. Hopefully he'll find that missing 'L' at some point.

"After years of struggling for funds we should be able to take advantage of paying for the stadium. And won't it be a relief to tell

1 Sometimes young aspiring Diarists ask us for our insights into the tough world of Diarism. So here's an example of just how tough things can get out here, on these mean streets. Towards the end of the editing process, mere hours before our first deadline, one of us accidentally replaced the words "Arsene Wenger and Ivan Gazidis" with a Youtube link to Dick Van Dyke singing "Chim Chim Cher-ee". This is not a life for the faint at heart.

the fans that we can definitely compete in the transfer market and not feel a hot sting of shame?

"Any problem?"

Gazidis: "No, all makes sense and easily achieved."

MANUEL PELLEGRINI AND FERRAN SORIANO

Pellegrini: "Our midfield has been one of the strongest features of the season, but there are reasons to reinforce. We need someone to replace Yaya Toure and Fernandinho, to be an upgrade on James Milner, and to replace Javi Garcia. Fernando has the ability to link up play but also offers more defensively than others in the midfield, which will free up Toure ahead of him. It also makes us less reliable on Toure should he decide that he didn't want a puppy for his birthday after all.

"Willy Caballero can offer genuine competition to Joe Hart when he's out of form or looking at himself in the mirror practising his smirk. Dropping him for Costel Pantilimon was a bit like cutting off your nose to spite your defensive solidity. I know Caballero from Malaga so it's a straightforward decision, plus he's called Willy, which is going to make any rush of blood to the head significantly more amusing.

"Any problem?"

Soriano: "No, all makes sense and easily achieved if we get started early."

JOSE MOURINHO AND MICHAEL EMENALO

Mourinho: "Didier Drogba will be a much better back-up than Fernando Torres, and Diego Costa will clearly be a much more effective striker than either of them. This is because he's actually good. There's perhaps a risk that he'll struggle to adapt, given that Eden Hazard and Oscar's interplay aren't quite the same as direct as the service he was used to at Atletico Madrid. However, we'll have a full pre-season to prepare for this, and adding Cesc Fabregas should provide adequate support if we need to play a little more straightforwardly. We'll offer a variety of threats in attack this year, which is a huge change from last year when we struggled to break down teams that weren't obligingly throwing themselves on the floor.

"We should also have the chance to refresh at the back. Thibaut Courtois is now the superior option to Petr Cech, and after years on loan at Atletico he will be prepared for the change. Cesar Azpilicueta will have a chance to establish himself at right-back now that Filipe Luis can provide balance on the left. In the middle, Ivanovic can now provide cover without exposing us, and Zouma will be able to learn from Terry and Cahill's partnership as Terry is phased out. And his name sounds a bit like "zoomer", so that's fun.

"Any problem?"

Emanelo: "No, all makes sense. We've been working on the transfers for months, we're cracked Financial Fair Play, and we're making good use of our contacts. And did you see how much PSG ponied up for David Luiz?"

BRENDAN RODGERS AND JOHN HENRY

"Brendan": "After the problems in defence last year, we can strengthen easily. Dejan Lovren will provide organisation and leadership in the centre, and Southampton share a similar style to us so he should adjust quickly. We'll be able to leave Kolo Toure, thankfully, as just a back up, and he'll be far more reliable than Daniel Agger, should he stay. On the right, Javier Manquillo cannot be any worse than Glen Johnson, and the same goes for Alberto Moreno on the left. Jon Flanagan means well, but he's basically a mascot.

"In midfield, Emre Can will have the chance to take over from Steven Gerrard. It was clear that last season our captain was close to spent on the pitch, even if he remains popular with the fans. We can buy Rickie Lambert to maintain our sentimental 'narrative' percentages. Lazar Markovic and Adam Lallana can be brought in quickly to provide attacking variety that we'll need after Suarez, in order to support Sturridge. Plus his name sounds a bit like "laser", which is cool.[2]

"Any problem?"

Henry: "I'm a businessman, not a posturing child with a glued-on beard, so it's easily sorted."

LOUIS VAN GAAL AND ED WOODWARD

Van Gaal: "OK, this is a massive year for us. Yes, we're out of the Champions League, and yes, there's a state of flux and change, but

2 Fair to say Liverpool did not impress this year. The committee have not done their job well for a few years now, but it seems that Brendan's assistants are carrying the can. At least, they were first in line for the sack. It's not that they are blameless — Rodgers has made some daft choices — but Rodgers is not alone when blame should be given for some of the rank, typically Liverpool, purchases made.

that's an advantage. Now is the time to focus on the league and maybe, perhaps, spring a surprise now that we're reinvigorated and refreshed. This is a chance to hit the ground running and plant some seeds on the scorched earth.

"I'm switching to three in defence, which will make us more defensively solid. Chris, Jonny and Phil will be fighting it out for two spots, but I'll need Thomas Vermaelen. Luckily you've been working on this signing for about six or seven months so that shouldn't be too difficult.

"Rafael is a good player, and a hugely attractive man who gets Manchester United, but he's not convincing. We need a new right-back, or better yet a right wing-back. Juan Cuadrado, yes. He's clearly available, as Fiorentina have said they are happy to sell, so with us, as you say, happy to spend the money, I expect we'll wrap this up swiftly too.

"Also, Daley Blind would be extremely useful as we wait for Kevin Strootman. He's versatile enough to play in defence, on the left and in midfield. He's said he wants to go, Ajax have explicitly said they will sell him. Alright, he's called "blind", but what kind of puerile buffoons waste their time making jokes about footballer's names? Marcos Rojo should be an easy one too. The third party will want a profit, and we've a good relationship with Sporting Lisbon — it should be simple. His name means "red"? I don't care.

"Finally, with Carrick injured for the start of the season, and playing like he's injured for the last two seasons, we'll need Ander to get an understanding with Arturo Vidal quickly. Juventus have been nudging him into a transfer request for months, and Vidal hasn't denied that he'd join. He's clearly angling for us to put in a bid. You say we're happy to break the transfer record, and he'd be far less than that.

"Any problems?

Woodward: "About this 'money'..."[3]

3 Turns out there was money, it just had hilarious consequences. Radamel Falcao's own teammates looked on at him, confused by his odd gait, not convinced he had a fully functioning knee. Angel Di Maria turned up, got burgled, then couldn't be bothered to do anything except a hilarious sending-off. Ander Herrera was inexplicably on the naughty step, Daley Blind was the new John O'Shea. Luke Shaw spent the season getting increasingly grubby and increasingly injured. Marcos Rojo existed. But! United failed to buy Thomas Vermaelen. So that's something.

AUGUST 23rd

Aston Villa 0-0 Newcastle
Chelsea 2-0 Leicester
Crystal Palace 1-3 West Ham
Everton 2-2 Arsenal
Southampton 0-0 West Bromwich
Swansea 1-0 Burnley

AUGUST 24th

Hull 1-1 Stoke
Sunderland 1-1 Manchester United
Tottenham 4-0 QPR

AUGUST 25th

Manchester City 3-1 Liverpool

In theory, there are people who watch the Premier League because they like football.

In practice, there are people who watch the Premier League who don't like football — nobody does, it just beats speaking to your loved ones — but have been cursed by circumstance to support one of the constituent clubs, and so have no choice but to have their moods dragged sometimes up but mostly down by the adequacies but mostly inadequacies of eleven or so men who should be good at their jobs but mostly aren't. It's a metaphor for politics. You are welcome for this satirical joke.[1]

This brings us neatly to Tottenham Hotspur.

Coming into this weekend, narrative[2] junkies were delighted with the prospect of the latest manager to the slaughter, Mauricio Pochettino, facing off against not just one but two of the men who preceded him to Daniel Levy's bloody chopping block. In the Queens Park Rangers dugout, Harry Redknapp; in the boxes above him, Glenn Hoddle. What better pairing to introduce Pochettino to the facts of his inevitable doom?

After all, this is Tottenham. This is the place where managers go to find themselves driven slowly and quietly mad. The last man, Tim Sherwood, was so consumed by the place that he tore all the sleeves off his jackets, leaving him with (a) nowhere to wear his heart

1 It actually gets worse with each reading.

2 That fucking word. More on this later.

and (b) a soul perpetually sustained by getting in and around the nebulous concept of banter. Before him, Andre Villas-Boas slowly disappeared from view, leaving just an empty beard with a growling voice to hem and haw and croak its way through the after-match interviews.

This is a dugout haunted by managerial failure. Juande Ramos and his slow transformation into a miserable tree. Christian Gross and his perfectly sensible, entirely reasonable decision to commute to work using public transport, which he ruined with a perfectly peculiar, entirely ridiculous decision to tell everybody about it while at the same time being suspiciously foreign. Ossie Ardiles and his five-man front-line.

Even Redknapp himself, who was actually quite good at the job, ruined everything by deciding he wanted a better one and ending up with nothing, not even the Champions League. (They didn't qualify, right? You are welcome for this joke, Arsenal fans.)

But if it's going to go wrong, well, it's not going wrong yet. Two games in to the season, and Tottenham haven't done anything Tottenham yet. Against West Ham last week, they weren't particularly great before Kyle Naughton's dismissal, were quite understandably concerned with damage limitation afterwards, and yet managed to steal a win right at the death.

Then, when QPR came to visit they took the chance, before their own fans, to stretch their legs and show a bit of style. Emmanuel Adebayor was vibrant, Nacer Chadli actually did things, and Erik Lamela was brilliant. It's almost like one season isn't enough time to judge a young footballer who has changed country and culture, struggled with injury, and had to deal with being managed by two men who aren't long for the job, one of whom is Tim Sherwood, who made Lamela carry around all those discarded sleeves in training.

All that said, QPR were obliging opponents. A team defined by Rio Ferdinand, a figure whose increasing decrepitude has required a shift in formation[3], resulting in the odd sight of a team playing three at the back in terms of defenders, yet only two at the back in terms of functioning pairs of legs. Presumably the appointment of Hoddle was intended to graft some tactical nous onto Redknapp's mateyness; instead, the side are playing with worst aspects of both men, a tactically chaotic rabble who don't look like they're having any fun.

3 A formation that ended up with him sitting on the subs bench or in the stadium.

But let's focus on Spurs. Two games in, and already Pochettino's side have shown that they can both nick off with the points in the face of adversity, and shred weak opposition when the opportunity presents itself. Two good habits for football teams to get themselves into. And though some might be concerned that the optimism might be ruined by their next Premier League opponents Liverpool, a side that last season spent one hundred and eighty minutes alternately laughing in and kicking in their face, even this represents an opportunity for Pochettino.

After all, it's not often that a manager gets to approach a game knowing that anything short of a five-goal shoeing will represent progress. Heady days. We're not saying that Spurs are going to win the league, but we are definitely saying that they're not going to win it in a slightly less disappointing manner than last time. And that is all that most of the Premier League can hope for.

Oh go on then. Spurs are definitely going to win the league.

AUGUST 30th

Burnley 0-0 Manchester United
Everton 3-6 Chelsea
Manchester City 0-1 Stoke
Newcastle 3-3 Crystal Palace
QPR 1-0 Sunderland
Swansea 3-0 West Bromwich
West Ham 1-3 Southampton

AUG 31st

Aston Villa 2-1 Hull
Leicester 1-1 Arsenal
Tottenham 0-3 Liverpool[1]

1 An improvement on 5-0. Congratulations Tottenham!

The Premier League is an odd business. One minute you're up, then you're down. Indeed, as Katy Perry put it: You change your mind like a girl changes clothes. Yeah, you, PMS like a bitch. I would know. And you over think, always speak, critically. 'Cause you're hot then you're cold. You're yes then you're no. You're in then you're out. You're up then you're down. You're wrong when it's right. It's black and it's white. You're hot then you're cold. You're yes then you're no. You're in then you're out. You're up then you're down.[2] Wise words, we think you'll agree. Wise words that you have been completely ignoring. We mean, well, just look at the state of you.

Then!

Louis van Gaal is a pragmatist, but favours an attacking 4-3-3 formation. With some sensible reinforcements, and the chance to continue his work with Robin van Persie, things are looking up. They should add Arturo Vidal, Daley Blind, Thomas Vermaelen, Luke Shaw and Ander Herrera. Van Gaal has given his transfer target list Edward Woodward and the Woodster — aka the Woodsman, Woody Woodington, Big Eddy Would — will be working on making sure they're all around for pre-season. It might be a tough situation for the manager, but he has experience on using plenty of different formations, and the World Cup has shown he can take an imbalanced squad and get them playing to its full potential. If

2 An introduction that looks amusing enough, but was definitely padding.

everything clicks then a run at the title, with the advantage of being out of Europe, is the bare minimum we can expect.

Now!

The pressure is building on Manchester United and Louis van Gaal, who is under increasing scrutiny from the press and executives. He's spent £150 million pounds on Marcos Rojo, Daley Blind, Ander Herrera, Luke Shaw and Angel Di Maria, and he still can't improve results. The formation has been terrible for four matches, and therefore must be changed. The defenders he has used have been utterly risible, and the injuries they've picked up have absolutely nothing to do with anything, frankly, and it's embarrassing that you've chosen to mention them. They've dropped points from the leaders already, with Chelsea winning all three of their games, but fourth now looks almost impossible. So does fifth. Tenth at best.

Then!

Roberto Martinez, Everton manager, is the man for whom Manchester United should have moved. His approach to the game is unfailingly attractive, and even Tom Cleverley is the kind of player that has previously blossomed under his tuition. With his shiny brown shoes and his brilliant eye for the loan deal — Romelu Lukaku, Gareth Barry and Gerard Deulofeu — he transformed Everton's long-ball cloggers into a blue, Merseyside Barcelona. If they hold on to Lukaku and Barry, and add sensibly — this Muhamed Besic was impressive at the World Cup — then they can't help but kick on.

Now!

It's all falling apart with Martinez at Everton as they suffer from the inevitable second season syndrome. His failure to invest in the defence has resulted in mistakes from veterans like Tim Howard and Sylvain Distin, players who know they are coming to the end of their careers but face no serious competition. And now Martinez is trying to buy Tom Cleverley[3] — there's absolutely no way a player like that could improve things. His other midfield purchase, Besic, used his first touch against Chelsea to backheel straight into John Obi Mikel's path, making him the proud owner of the world's first recorded negative pass completion percentage. Worse than that,

3 And now he's got him on a free transfer. The great thing about Cleverley is he isn't bad, he just gives everyone reasons to dislike and mock him.

Martinez has spent £28 million on a striker who has a miserable first touch and is showing why Jose Mourinho didn't trust him. Things are looking difficult for Everton now. Tenth at best.

Then!
Doom at Aston Villa. Doom with a capital DOO-DOO-DOO. Randy Lerner wants out, and the only question is whether he gets out before his underinvestment guarantees relegation this season or next. The signings have been utterly desperate. Kieran Richardson, an utter failure at Fulham, and Lord Snooty to his erstwhile Manchester United fans. Philippe Senderos is back after being part of that same Fulham side, and then joining Valencia for eight unimpressive games. Aly Cissokho, not trusted by Brendan Rodgers to improve even the ropey Liverpool defence last season, has been joined by Alan Hutton, previously and correctly frozen out by manager Paul Lambert. Worse than that, Joe Cole is there, having last played well for a few games in Lille. Roy Keane has joined, but clearly as a stalking, bearded horse — how can Lambert work under such pressure?

Now!
A remarkable turnaround. Randy Lerner's openness about his plans to sell has let everyone know where they stand and plan accordingly. Roy Keane[4] has worked excellently to instill discipline on the young players, and rejuvenate the veterans brought in on free transfers or out from the cold. These shrewd investments have brought in Premier League nous without Premier League transfer fees. Aston Villa have now got a bright future ahead of them, with stability, and the chance that a new owner will be tempted to take over and finally give Lambert the funds to kick on to the next level[5]. They've got the eyes of the tiger, a fighter, dancing through the fire. They're going to finish tenth, and you're gonna hear them roaaaaaaaaaaaaaaar.

4 A particularly big Cleverley fan, who ended up visiting the midfielder's house to confront him over suspicions that he was leaking team news. Good bloke, is Tom.

5 They actually gave him a new contract. Then they sacked him. Well done all round.

SEPTEMBER 3rd

England 1-0 Norway

SEPTEMBER 8th

Switzerland 0-2 England[1]

SEPTEMBER 13th

Arsenal 2-2 Manchester City

Chelsea 4-2 Swansea

Crystal Palace 0-0 Burnley

Liverpool 0-1 Aston Villa

Southampton 4-0 Newcastle

Stoke 0-1 Leicester

Sunderland 2-2 Tottenham

West Bromwich 0-2 Everton

SEPTEMBER 14th

Manchester United 4-0 QPR

SEPTEMBER 15th

Hull 2-2 West Ham

SEPTEMBER 20th

Aston Villa 0-3 Arsenal

Burnley 0-0 Sunderland

Newcastle 2-2 Hull

QPR 2-2 Stoke

Swansea 0-1 Southampton

West Ham 3-1 Liverpool

SEPTEMBER 21st

Everton 2-3 Crystal Palace

Leicester 5-3 Manchester United

Manchester City 1-1 Chelsea

Tottenham 0-1 West Bromwich

1 We forgot to write up this weekend on the following Monday. We then were reminded, and forgot again on the Tuesday.

Ahead of Manchester United's routine victory over Leicester City, Louis van Gaal explained his decision to move Wayne Rooney further back into the team and give him the number 10 position. He explained that "I was not so satisfied with Rooney as a striker," and that Rooney had told him that it was his best position.

Then followed an interview with the man himself, Manchester United's captain. He said "I'm happy to play out wide; I can do a job there and I can do a job up front. I'm not the player I was ... I feel like I've progressed my game. I done too much running when I was younger. I'm a cleverer player now and know when to run into the box and when not to, and as a result more chances have come my way."[2]

Which is a change from the 5th of June 2013, when he said: "In the years to come, that might be somewhere I could play, but, right now, I'm definitely a centre-forward. I'm after more goals, I've played up front on my own a few times for Manchester United and it's a role I'm very comfortable with and have no problems playing." A little over a year ago Rooney had decided his best position was as a striker. This was when his scoring went.

Which follows, because a couple of months before then, whether or not he did indeed ask for a transfer or not, everyone seems to agree that Rooney had discussed with Alex Ferguson his reluctance to be

2 It was his worst season ever, his touch deserted him, as did his creativity and shooting boots. He emphatically proved he could not play as a number 10, and yet there he is, captain Rooney.

played, as he saw it, out of position for Manchester United. This was when his first touch went.

Which was a transfer request, or at least a transfer insinuation, which followed the arrival of Robin van Persie and his usurping of Rooney as the very best striker United had. When Shinji Kagawa had been bought the same season with the intention, though aborted, of replacing Rooney. This was when his confidence went.

Which were transfers which came a couple of years after Rooney had demanded to leave Manchester United in October 2010, supposedly with the intention of forcing through a move to Manchester City, who wanted to bloody the nose of United and prove they were the biggest club in Manchester and in all of the Premier League. By meeting his own ambition and winning the Premier League, Ferguson had rendered Rooney's obsolete. This was when his passing went.

In 2010 Rooney wanted to leave and he was rewarded with an increased wage and a league title in 2011. In 2012/13 Rooney was given Robin van Persie as competition, came off worse, and supposedly asked that despite that, he be played in his best position as a striker and/or be sold. In 2013/14 Rooney said he was definitely a centre-forward, tried to leave for Chelsea, and was given a five year-contract, A wage that can reach £300,000 a week thanks to United's pride of all Europe commercial operation, along with, apparently, special access to the club's prospective signings. He scored 16 times. In 2014/15 Wayne Rooney was made captain, the club bought Radamel Falcao and he decided he was now a number 10, having seen that his competition for striker was Van Persie and Falcao, and concluded that Juan Mata would be easier to displace. This is when his usefulness went.

In the 43rd minute against Leicester, Rooney ran straight into Esteban Cambiasso. In the 64th minute, Rooney passed to a Leicester player on the edge of United's box and, A few moments later, Cambiasso scored. At which point Rooney responded by shouting at all the players around him. In the 83rd minute Leicester scored their fifth from the penalty spot and Rooney was booked for dissent. Bar one assist, Rooney had yet another appalling match in which he failed in his duties as both footballer and captain, however you might choose to divide those.

He failed to offer encouragement to the young players and the new team that is being built. He failed to find any spark that might inspire his side to make a comeback/stop Leicester making their comeback. A team that is built around him after being excluded from playing up front — remember: "I'm definitely a centre-forward"

— and he deciding he is now a number 10. He can't run, he can't pass, he can't shoot and he can't lead. We can only assume that Van Gaal, in giving him the armband, is simultaneously handing Rooney plenty of rope, fastened just so into a noose. Here you go, Wayne. Your best position, the responsibility of captaincy, and the best attacking teammates the world has to offer. Show us what you can do. Oh. Oh dear.

To paraphrase his nemesis Alex Ferguson's favourite bed sheet: three years of excuses and it's still crap. Ta-ra, Rooney?

***

In other Manchester United news, Mario Balotelli made fun of them because they were intensely, truly mockable; so bad that even a striker who lost to West Ham the day before was perfectly entitled to have a pop. United fans responded with countless racist tweets as a result, which will make the next Suarez joke from the very same people ring fairly hollow.

***

In other Manchester City news, Pablo Zabaleta has claimed that Diego Costa[3] should have been sent off, essentially using the argument that he started it, anyway. Zabaleta is 29.

3 Easily the biggest arsehole in the league, but not the worst person.

SEPTEMBER 27th

Arsenal 1-1 Tottenham
Chelsea 3-0 Aston Villa
Crystal Palace 2-0 Leicester
Hull 2-4 Manchester City
Liverpool 1-1 Everton
Manchester United 2-1 West Ham
Southampton 2-1 QPR
Sunderland 0-0 Swansea

SEPTEMBER 28th

West Bromwich 4-0 Burnley

SEPTEMBER 29th

Stoke 1-0 Newcastle

It was all set up so perfectly. Four teams who could not, by any real stretch of the imagination, be considered to be in CRISIS, but who are each definitely in PRE-CRISIS, an ominous limbo state in which disaster hasn't yet arrived but is only a couple of bad results away, in which everything hasn't gone all wrong but it's easy to see just how it might. Two from Merseyside, playing one another; two from north London, likewise. CRISIS, surely, was inevitable.

Hopes were high for the early kickoff. After all, Liverpool against Everton was a match between two teams who view defending as something between an unpleasant chore — but *boss*, I want to go and do a *goal*, everybody else gets to go and do *goals*, it's not *fair* — and a completely alien concept. When the really quite movable object meets the other really quite movable object, it makes sense to assume that the winner will come from the odd goal in thirteen. And that the loser will come out of the other side in a right state.

Instead, competence.

Liverpool were the slightly better team, as befits the slightly stronger team playing at home, while Everton weren't as good but kept things close enough that Jagielka could tap home a late equaliser. Defenders resolutely refused to run into each other, to punch themselves in the face, to ignore their goalkeeper's instructions, though Mamadou Sakho's reputation took another hit when he was instructed to closely mark a seat in the director's box and ending up accidentally leaving the stadium. Everton tried to play sensibly and did okay, as did Liverpool. Nobody got sent off; only one person should have been. And when the feistiest player on the pitch is Gareth Barry, for God's sake, you know something's gone wrong.

But surely — surely — the north London derby would deliver later in the day. After all, Arsenal may be unbeaten in the league but they've also been profoundly unconvincing, a strange confection of bad luck, risible defending, and completely weird squad balancing. Tottenham, meanwhile, have been struggling to raise their game above the workmanlike. Either an Arsenal implosion or a Tottenham surrender was coming, it was just a question of who hiccuped first. And whoever would, well, misery was certain to follow.

Instead, tightness.

Arsenal did their part, turning in a performance of concentrated, distilled Arsenal; attractive but weirdly un-incisive attacking laced with two inexplicable and important injuries, Mathieu Flamini being total rubbish, and Danny Welbeck inadvertently setting up a goal by missing the ball completely and tackling himself to the ground in the process. But Tottenham unexpectedly manufactured some backbone in defence and got their pressing on in attack, the standout moments being a blinding save by Hugo Lloris and some decent hustle by Christian Eriksen. Actually, the real standout moment was Erik Lamela's hideous slice that set up Arsenal's equaliser, but it would be cruel to mention that.

So what happened, overall? Ultimately, both home teams will feel a little vexed not to have taken all three points, while both away teams will feel quite pleased to have got their one. More importantly, all four teams stayed clear of CRISIS, at least for another week. But does this mean they are out of PRE-CRISIS? Most assuredly not. Because we'll let you into a little secret here: all Premier League teams are in PRE-CRISIS, all the time. That's how the game works. If a team's not yet in a mess, then it's about to be. Or it's Chelsea. Congratulations on the title, Jose.[1]

***

Finally, a note for Super Sunday's high-octane clash, in which West Bromwich Albion shredded Burnley. Not on the game — which can be summed up by the fact that Sky Sports spent most of the time telling viewers to flip over to the golf — but on the touchlines. We at the Diary would like to suggest to football managers that they

1 And for next season.

consult with the freelance writing community before deciding on their wardrobe.

Our reasoning is this: both Sean Dyche and Alan Irvine look like police officers from some ITV drama series. Dyche, a hulking figure with an aggressively groomed beard, is the very image of a patient, by-the-book detective inspector, the kind of copper who asks question after obstinate question, slowly edging his way towards some kind of solution.

Irvine, meanwhile, has a sharper face and a snippy presence; he's the kind of officer who trusts his instincts but has little time for procedure or paperwork, an attitude that occasionally gets him in trouble with his superiors. But not that much trouble. It's not like many officers of any level play by the rules, is it?

So a bit of coordination could have delivered to the weary viewer a minor piece of diversionary entertainment, a classic straight cop-maverick cop combo on the sidelines. The fourth official, by juxtaposition, would start to look like a local businessman whose name keeps turning up in the strangest of places.

Dyche would amble over and mutter something — in the real world, about an offside decision — and ask him to remember, just one more time, where he was on the evening of August 12th. Then Irvine would go over — perhaps a foul hadn't been given on the far side — and scream "Look! We know you did it! Now tell us where the body is or we'll do something that isn't really isn't in line with PACE!"

It would have been diverting. It would have been mildly amusing for a few seconds. It would have been significantly more fun than the game. And all it would have taken was Irvine to check with us, see what we were thinking, then wear a suit. Instead, he turned up in trackies, and an entire riff was dead before it even got off the ground. Think of the people that really matter, Alan. Think of the Diary writers.

OCTOBER 4th

Aston Villa 0-2 Manchester City
Hull 2-0 Crystal Palace
Leicester 2-2 Burnley
Liverpool 2-1 West Bromwich
Sunderland 3-1 Stoke
Swansea 2-2 Newcastle

OCTOBER 5th

Chelsea 2-0 Arsenal
Manchester United 2-1 Everton
Tottenham 1-0 Southampton
West Ham 2-0 QPR

Arsene Wenger wakes up at 8am. He switches off his alarm and reaches an arm across to his wife in bed. She is not there. Realising, from the sounds in the kitchen downstairs, that she is already awake, he goes downstairs, smelling the coffee scents emanating from below. Still blurry-eyed, he pours from the cafetiere into his favourite mug, but cannot work out why there is no coffee.

"Oh, sorry darling," says his wife. "I just finished it off." Slightly surprised that she doesn't offer to make him a new one, despite having taking all the coffee for herself, Wenger goes to the sink, fills up the kettle and set about preparing another round. "Oh thanks Arsene," says his wife. "I'd love another."

Hearing his stomach rumble, he turns to the fridge, takes out the butter from the top shelf, and put on a couple of slices of toast. He removes the jam from the second shelf down and hovers over the toaster, waiting to grab the bread at exactly the right time. Until, that is, he hears the kettle pop, at which point he heads over and fills the cafetiere with water, attaching the plunger.

"Oh, merde!"[1] he exclaims, as he smells the bread burning in the toaster. As he runs across to rescue the toast before it becomes inedible, he catches his toe on the corner of the kitchen island. He curses his luck.

"Are you OK, Arsene?" asks his wife.

"NO I'M NOT FUC-yes, dear, sorry, thanks, just some bad luck,"

1 Yes, we're fluent.

Wenger replies, catching himself before he completely loses his temper. He finally sits down with his coffee and blackened toast, which is now not warm enough to melt the butter properly. The coffee has a slightly stale taste from being left out for too long, and is weaker than usual. He realises that the plunger had made its own way down, ahead of schedule, and that he's been meaning to get a new one for ages.

Breakfasted, after a fashion, Wenger heads to the bathroom to get ready for the match. He steps into the shower and turns on the taps, and waits for the hot water to come through. And waits. And waits. And waits. Lukewarm. He remembers the last gas engineer saying that a valve needed replacing soon, and he remembers forgetting to get around to it. So Wenger stands there for a few minutes, shivering slightly under the tepid water as a draft whips in from the loose window in the bathroom. Should get that looked at, he thinks. He decides against washing his hair in the cold water, and steps out. His hair still has that slightly irritating, unwashed feel.

Back in the bedroom, cold and mostly dry, Wenger takes the dry-cleaned club suit out of the wardrobe and shuffles through the coathangers looking for a white shirt to wear. He had torn the cuff of his favourite one last week after catching it on a door handle, and so looks for another, eventually settling on his fourth-favourite, which is crumpled but looks clean enough. He sets up the ironing board, plugs in the iron, and lays the shirt out carefully on the board. He sprays some water onto the shirt from the iron and begins to draw the iron across the wrinkled fabric, hitting the steam button as he goes. The puffing clouds feel pleasantly warm.

As he turns the shirt over to do the other side, he notices a small orange-ish stain on the shirt, and realises it has come from a little bit of rust on the iron. He gets as far as "Oh, MOTHERFU-" before he stops himself, realising that it's okay, that it's just a shirt. He puts on a t-shirt underneath his suit, knowing he can buy another along the way to the ground.

Getting onto the Arsenal coach, slightly tired around the eyes, slightly greasy around the hair, and five minutes late because his wife had lost her joint account card and taken his, which meant he'd been unable to use it for his new shirt at M&S, and it had taken him ages to remember the PIN[2] for his credit card, he sees his players clicking on their iPhones, having not turned off the input sound on

2 Is the worst thing about Twitter the number of people who point out 'PIN number' is tautologous? Indeed it is.

the keyboards. He hears two of them playing the same song on their headphones, slightly out of time with one another. He takes a deep breath and remembers he must keep calm for his players and allow them to prepare as they want.

As he gives the final team talk in the away dressing room, he notices Lukas Podolski taking a selfie, distracting a couple of players around him, giggling at a joke he makes. He tells Podolski sharply that "if you can't behave, you can stand outside 'til I'm done," then immediately regrets his outburst and apologises. He wishes all his players luck and gives a few final instructions, and they walk out onto the pitch. He takes his seat in the dugout. He doesn't mention that Steve Bould is, once again, sitting with his legs uncomfortably wide, encroaching on Wenger's own leg space.

Fifteen minutes into the game, Gary Cahill slides into Alexis Sanchez with a reckless and dangerous challenge on the touchline. Wenger had expected this: it was Phil Neville on Jose Antonio Reyes all over again, and he isn't surprised. But then he remembers the coffee, the toast, the shower, the draft from the window. He winces as his stubbed toe flares with pain, he runs his hand through his claggy hair, and he sees that he hasn't taken the size sticker off his new shirt. Embarrassed, tetchy and furious, he storms towards Jose Mourinho, saying in his head, "I'm gonna hit him I'm gonna hit him I'm gonna hit him I'm gonna hit him I'm gonna hit him."

And he gives him a little shove.[3]

3 For which he was not banned. Which, of course he shouldn't have been, but it ably demonstrates how subjective the FA are in dealing with certain players and managers. Had Mourinho done the same thing, he'd have been banned for three games and be making handcuff gestures on Goals on Sunday. Think of what Ben Shepherd would have made of that.

OCTOBER 9th

England 5-0 San Marino

OCTOBER 12th

Estonia 0-1 England

There are times — don't you find? — when you just want to reach out to Roy Hodgson, grasp his hand firmly, look him directly in the eye and say: Thank you. Thank you for being who you are. Thank you for being the most Roy Hodgson-esque Roy Hodgson imaginable.[1] Thank you.

Raheem Sterling, apparently, was tired. We know this because Roy Hodgson told us so; apparently Sterling approached him after training and said "Look I really am feeling a little tired, I am not in my best form at the moment because I am feeling a bit tired."

The first thing to note is that you can really hear the influence of Brendan Rodgers in there. "Not in my best form" is a lovely Rodgersian construction, an extension of a common phrase — "in form" — that sounds at once smoothly plausible and yet faintly alien. For some people, form is a binary state: you're in it or you not. Not for Brendan's charges, though. Where is your best form, and how do you get in there? What is the framework of your best form and how do you get in and around the framework, which I encourage you to do. There's almost certainly a journey to be made. To the stationery shop ...

That's assuming that Hodgson reported the right words in the right order, of course, which might be a touch generous. This is a man who tells jokes punchline first, after all, and we don't think he

1 At the time of writing, he is currently annoyed at ITV for tweeting that the deathly boring game between Ireland and England was, indeed, boring.

was attempting to locate new levels of humour through subverting the mechanics of the form. Perhaps it's best to treat these quotes as advisory.

So, to business. Is this a bad thing? Sorry, hang on. Is this A Bad Thing, this admission of fatigue, this self-diagnosis? Obviously it is. Any time a footballer feels tired, they should immediately think to themselves 'What would our brave boys in the forces do?' Then they should join the army. Sorry, hang on. Then they should just get on with the football. Far better to pretend not to be tired, to play badly, and to possibly pick up an injury. That way lies true commitment. That way lies real bravery. Did St George let a bit of peakiness get in the way of his glorious mission to murder endangered species? Did he heck as like. Did Winston Churchill ever stop drinking port and brandy and smoking cigars just because he was ill?[2] No! Like a proper Englishman, he kept right on going until he actually died.

This next paragraph was going to be about Raheem Sterling's increased workload this season, both physically (as an established first-team player in a side returning to European football) and mentally (as, thanks to Daniel Sturridge's injury, he's suddenly become the most important attacking player in a side that hasn't really got going). But then, it doesn't really matter. If Sterling[3] said something, then he did so either because he was feeling that way, or because he simply couldn't be arsed facing Estonia. Hard to blame him, in either case, but we can probably assume the former. And if so, then there's not really much to be done. We're not doctors, but it doesn't seem plausible that energy can be restored by saying "nope, you should have more energy". That seems like it might just be annoying.

(As an aside, one might even suggest that for a player within the hyper-macho world of professional sport, true bravery lies in being able to recognise one's occasional moments of not being a super-charged super-capable super-optimum athlete. That in a culture that places unthinking commitment above all other virtues, being willing to acknowledge one's own mortality is, in its own way, significantly more courageous than just "manning up". But we digress.)

2 If you do not enjoy this book, then please keep in mind that we were tired but nonetheless kept going out of respect to you, the reader, and the armed forces.

3 Sterling later outraged Liverpool fans by asking to leave because he wasn't paid very much and Liverpool were rubbish again. He outraged nobody by having the exact opposite facial hair coverage of Seth Armstrong from Emmerdale Farm. That's right, Farm.

Maybe it was all psychological; maybe a better leader of men than Hodgson could have put his arm around Sterling's shoulders and, with a few choice quotations from Henry V, restored the vim and vigour to his limbs. (For the record, the V in Henry V actually stands for Vimto. Not quite vim or vigour, but an encouraging noun nonetheless, to some.)

But as solutions go, leaving him on the bench doesn't seem particularly inelegant. Somebody else gets a game, the players learn that Hodgson will listen to their concerns, and chances are England are going to be able to squeak past Estonia without Sterling. Oh look, they did.

As for why he mentioned it to the wider world? A cynic might suggest that he did so in response to the fallout from the last international break — ah! such memories! we were all so young and innocent back then — when he ostentatiously failed to listen to one of his players[4] and ended up breaking them. A cynic might well be right. As PR techniques go, hilarious self-aggrandisement is just about superior to insulting your captain's speaking voice, so at least we can say that Hodgson improved as the week went on.

But perhaps Hodgson has a nobler goal in mind. Were he not quite so wonderfully, perfectly, beautifully Roy Hodgson, there's every chance England — the team, the nation, the state of mind — might have just recorded the world's first entirely frictionless international break. In one end and, two unspectacular but extremely fibrous results later, out the other. Nothing to talk about. Nothing to think about. Nothing to engage with, no lessons to learn.[5] We know from every other summer what happens when England has no football to engage with: the entire country suffers a collective episode and starts pretending that Wimbledon is good. Imagine what might happen if England were left bereft and there was no tennis on.

No. Bless the Almighty Hodge, for he is here to help. Where there is nothing, let him sow something. Where nobody gives a toss, give them something to give a toss about. If Fabio Capello brought organisation and Steve McClaren bought sensible policies for dealing with rain when attempting to take notes, then this is what Hodgson brings to the England table: the unerring ability

4 Daniel Sturridge. You have to admire Hodgson's dedication to making Liverpool fans miserable.

5 And yet somehow we still managed to craft this outstanding chapter from it. Which is an improvement on the first international break, when we simply forgot to write about it.

to lash his own foot into his own mouth from 30 yards, literally.

In a country with a media that works the way this one's does, there is no skill more valuable. Thank you, Roy. Without you, we'd be lost.

OCTOBER 18th

Arsenal 2-2 Hull
Burnley 1-3 West Ham
Crystal Palace 1-2 Chelsea
Everton 3-0 Aston Villa
Manchester City 4-1 Tottenham
Newcastle 1-0 Leicester
Southampton 8-0 Sunderland

OCTOBER 19th

QPR 2-3 Liverpool
Stoke 2-1 Swansea

OCTOBER 20th

West Bromwich 2-2 Manchester United

When a new technological or other invention is released in its first iteration, it is usually larger than the model or appearance that comes to define it. The first iPod was far larger than those that followed, as more and more songs could be stored on a smaller and smaller storage system. Paracetamol tablets were originally the size of crisps, but modern technology shrank them down to a more useable size. More recently, to save on transportation costs, things like squash and washing detergent have become 'double concentrate', allowing the dilution to be done at the user end. That the user always forgets, ends up making undrinkably strong squash, and rattles through the bottle at double speed is just a coincidence, we're sure (that's right, Radio 4's You And Yours[1], we're coming for your crown).

But it's not just in the world of commerce that this process takes place. With time and effort, football can become ever more concentrated and refined into its purest forms. Take Arsenal, for example. Arsene Wenger is called The Professor for a reason — his scientific ability to make Arsenal the most Arsenal per pound they can scientifically be.

It's a process that takes a number of steps — indeed, it's been his life's work — but this summer and the start of the season demonstrates

1 Earlier this season, we considered what the worst thing on Radio 4 was. A few suggestions: Saturday Live, Broadcasting House, Kitchen Cabinet [interestingly, **** **** once called one of our friends a **** via email], and You And Yours. Oh, and The News Quiz. Gardener's Question Time, though, is oddly soothing.

that clear decisions have been taken, and we're getting ever close to the perfect state of Zen-like Arsenal.

1) Jack Wilshere is becoming more of an English footballer than ever before

The signs were always there. The St George's day poem, the iffy declarations of who qualifies as English, and the picture of him lying on a Union Jack sofa with a bulldog on his chest. If you wanted to define 'obvious subtext' you would do so with Jack Wilshere's way of life. This is a man who wears his nationality on his sleeve, just above the space where the Brave And Noble Captain's armband will one day surely rest.

Wilshere broke on the scene at 17, with exceptional poise for someone so young and with an eye for a pass rarely seen in someone with a passport granted by this country's home office. He sadly, though, also possessed ankles like Kim Jong Un, and has spent his career hamstrung by injury. though not to his hamstrings, at least not yet. And, as he acknowledged after criticism from Paul Scholes last season, he had not progressed sufficiently. Everybody thought this was a reference to becoming a footballer; Wilshere knew otherwise.

And so in little over an hour, he had whittled his performance into a microcosm of both club and nation. Running around, falling over injured, sending through balls too short of his man, pushing players over with his stubby little arms like Gazza, and then hurtling into a reckless tackle and damaging his knee. Applauded off? You bet. Wenger has spoken of the need to re-Englishify Arsenal, and here's proof that he's going the right way about it. 100% bulldog and 95% Arsenal By Volume.[2]

2) Nacho Monreal at centre back

Thomas Vermaelen, he wasn't very good. Thomas Vermaelen, he scored lots of goals and was at least a central defender of some years. Thomas Vermaelen, he almost went to Manchester United but then he went to Barcelona. Whatever the opinions on his ability and balsa-wood nature, he was a senior player and the tradition is that when you sell one, you replace one. Unless you're Arsenal, in

2 The great thing about Arsenal is that if you're even mildly critical about them, hordes of artisan-croissant-swilling internet turds will send you tweets hoping your mum dies. Not your mum, obviously. You know what we mean.

which case you take a child from Southampton[3], tell Hector Bellerin to get warmed up for the season, and decide arbitrarily that Nacho Monreal can do a job there anyway.

If you then concede a goal by one man strolling through the centre of the pitch, and then one from a cross when nobody bothers marking, you can rate yourself 80% ABV.

3) Promise investment in January

Wenger has said he will now buy a central defender in January. Confiture demain. 60% ABV.

4) Look mortally affronted at fairly routine questions

Wenger gets an easy ride in most press conferences. Although he is foreign, he's not treated with surly contempt by a certain set of hacks. Because he has been around for two decades, and he doesn't ban journalists like the previous time-served champion, Alex Ferguson, he is treated as if he is a thoroughly decent man, and there is palpable reluctance to go for the jugular to his face. Pro tip: if you actually want to go for the jugular, attack from behind. The element of surprise is key. How do we know that?[4] Only God can judge us.

It's understandable, but it isn't really fair on other managers. They are regularly provoked into amusing tantrums for the benefit of the public and the online journalists who scrape a living by mocking those people who actually do a hard job that requires qualifications and discipline.

Well, no longer. Finally, Jacqui Oatley dared to ask Arsene Wenger who was to blame for the pathetic display against Hull. (For the record, the answer is Arsene Wenger; this is so much his club that they've named it after him). Wenger reacted as if he was being asked to take blame for the death of a family member in a tragic accident, rather than a draw at home. For too long Wenger has been treated as if he is special, and as a result Arsenal now truly believe they are the London Barcelona. Their astonishing reaction to utterly logical questions? 100% ABV

3 This great moral club, Arsenal, have just been charged due to alleged improper agent action in the transfer. Truly, the mini-Barcelona.

4 Growing up on the mean streets of Tunbridge Wells.

OCTOBER 25th

West Ham 2-1 Manchester City

Liverpool 0-0 Hull

Southampton 1-0 Stoke

Sunderland 0-2 Arsenal

West Bromwich 2-2 Crystal Palace

Swansea 2-0 Leicester

OCTOBER 26th

Burnley 1-3 Everton

Tottenham 1-2 Newcastle

Manchester United 1-1 Chelsea

OCTOBER 27th

QPR 2-0 Aston Villa

There are many compelling and enjoyable things about Louis van Gaal. His face, for one. His barely-concealed contempt for everybody that doesn't agree with him, for two. And, for three, his magnificent ability to relieve himself all over the chips of even those footballers he apparently loves more than the rest:

"He did a stupid reaction after the goal. You can be excited but you don't have to pull your shirt off because then you have a yellow card. It is not so smart."

The headlines have led with "stupid" but the real joy there is "not so smart," a beautifully dismissive turn of phrase. He was right, too, and not just about the booking. Robin van Persie, by equalising late on, ruined absolutely everything. For everybody. The reason that you have a headache, that you didn't get enough sleep, that your Monday morning is a maelstrom of chaos and flux? Blame Robin.

A few lousy seconds. Just a few lousy seconds more, and then Chelsea would have had their win and we could have stuck a fork in the Premier League. Strange phrase, that one. Surely the fork is stuck in not to celebrate the fact of something being done, but to check whether it is done? It should really be "Observe the juices running clear, it's done," though you can understand why that's never really caught on. Vegetables do not have juices, exactly. And "Take the fork out, carve it up, then stick another fork, or possibly the same one, unless the juices weren't running clear the first time, because food poisoning is not fun, back in for the purposes of consumption," is a bit unwieldy.

Anyway, that's all beside the point. (Don't know why you brought it up, to be honest.) The point is: Van Persie took what would have been a tidy future and messed it all up. Any late result-shifting goal kills off the match reports, of course, and the pre-written light-hearted Diary entries[1], but in this case the whole country was set to proclaim Chelsea champions. With City losing earlier in the weekend; with Arsenal, United, Tottenham and Liverpool looking various shades of inadequate; with their nearest competition coming from Southampton and West Ham.

We, all of us, could have basically written off the top of the table for the rest of the season. Think how much more relaxed things would be. Super Sundays could be set aside for long walks in the crisp winter air, or peaceful sessions in cosy pubs, or finally getting around to putting those shelves up, or watching Aston Villa. Footballing attention could be devoted to leagues where the cast and crew aren't quite so irritating. Get along to the local team. Go and watch Dulwich Hamlet. Ignore the top of the world's loudest league. Avoid the headaches. Only check in every few weeks or so to see if Jose Mourinho is on track to claim his final triumph over Arsene Wenger by going unbeaten all season but with slightly fewer draws.

But no. Robin had to go and lash one home from a few yards and keep us all wondering for another few weeks. And the worst thing? In essence, nothing has really changed. The league's already done, and Chelsea are winning the thing. Yet now we have to spend a whole 'nother week pretending to care about 'the title race'. Good work, Robin. Good work. Not so smart, indeed. Don't let those forks out of your sight just yet though.

Chelsea's coronation party — cancelled at the last minute due to a cutlery shortage — was only coming because Manchester City once again pulled off a Manchester City. At least, that's what people are saying. In truth, however, this result owed little to City's peculiar finishing and defensive inadequacies, and more, much more, to the return of one of modern football's true heroes.

There are people in this universe who profess not to enjoy the sight of Allardyce in full pomp. These people are lying to themselves. Football has many pleasures to offer the not-quite-yet-totally-jaded, but the best and most noble must surely be the sight of a nominally superior side being undone by a theoretical inferior. And nobody does

1 Each chapter takes hours. Sometimes we don't sleep on Sunday to make sure that our opinions come to you in perfect shape.

that better or with more relish than Allardyce. Some managers get up the nose of the big beasts; Allardyce, once he's up there, capers around shouting and stamping his feet. "I'm up your nose! I'm up your nose! Have some of that! I'm up your nose! Give me the England job, you bastards."

The corollary to this is that like the little girl with the curl, when Allardyce is bad, he's horrid. Hideous, ineffective football, overseen by a grouchy, malfunctioning ego. Nothing enjoyable for anybody, particularly not those poor sods burdened by supporting the team he's squatting upon. No, the Premier League needs a good Allardyce team. It irks the purists, it inconveniences the aristocrats, and it really, really annoys Arsenal fans, still bearing the scars from the glory days of Bolton elbowing their way to sixth. Welcome back, big, irritating Sam. God's in his heaven, and all's right with the world. Now, please can we get him Rafael Benitez[2] back for Christmas?

2 Hilariously he now manages Real Madrid. Our predicted Benitez Real XI: Reina; Johnson, Coentrao, Pepe, Carvalho; Kroos, Tiote, Lucas; Gerrard; Cavani, Ronaldo.

NOVEMBER 1st

Newcastle 1-0 Liverpool
Arsenal 3-0 Burnley
Chelsea 2-1 QPR
Everton 0-0 Swansea
Hull 0-1 Southampton
Leicester 0-1 West Bromwich
Stoke 2-2 West Ham

NOVEMBER 2nd

Manchester City 1-0 Manchester United
Aston Villa 1-2 Tottenham

NOVEMBER 3rd

Crystal Palace 1-3 Sunderland

Football, it often seems, is obsessed with noting nice touches, lovely gestures, and classy acts from clubs, fans and players. These acts are sometimes used as a defence when football comes in for criticism from those who hold the sport in contempt, rugby fans who are proud of the fact that nobody swears at their referees, or clucking social commentators who see only young fools being foolish with their money. That football, footballers and football fans are capable of being decent human beings should be a surprise to nobody, of course, yet one of the most striking is also largely unremarked. We're talking about the generally accepted nods of respect from football to the armed forces.

Minute's silences took place at grounds around the country this weekend gone and they will also take place next weekend, as each club takes the opportunity to mark Remembrance Sunday at their home ground. It is not wrong to observe the silences, nor is it wrong to give each fan the chance to observe a silence at a match. But there is, nevertheless, something that has started to go wrong in this country as a whole, and as such finds itself inevitably reflected in the tone of English football's gestures. Remembrance Sunday is being conflated with a more general celebration of militarism, to the extent that even veterans of World War Two have started to shun the poppy.

Now, this is no attack on Remembrance Sunday. Those who died and served in World Wars One and Two deserve to have their contribution recognised by the state and the public. Conscription forced a great many people into facing real horrors at the behest of those in charge, and these wars — the Second World War especially — is one that Britain can be justified in believing it was better for the world that it was on the victorious side. A minute's silence at football grounds on the weekends around Armistice Day is, perhaps uniquely for football, almost entirely unobjectionable.

But it is harder, and might even be impossible, to say the same about Britain's more recent military activities. In an age of Iraq and Afghanistan, it cannot be assuredly said that those who were sacrificed by the state were doing so in missions that improved the lot of the world generally, the countries that were involved specifically, and the people who fought and died in those countries.

The FA wish to keep politics out of English football, just as FIFA wishes to do the same with the international game. On some level, that is a sensible way of trying to limit violence in and around football grounds. There are enough derbies or rivalries which are marked by political disputes between right and left, sectarianism, class hatred, and there are sometimes fights over the countries themselves. Look at Ireland vs England a couple of decades ago; look at Serbia vs Albania a few weeks back. It is clearly incredibly difficult to keep politics out of football, when almost everybody's life brings politics into football by virtue of us all having to live in the world, but it does however make sense to try to limit its potentially explosive nature.

According to who you believe, about two million people marched against the Iraq war. More recently, MPs decided not to back David Cameron when he tried to raise support for an intervention in Syria to act in the civil war (before Isis became well known). The Falklands remains a sore point for both countries, and Margaret Thatcher acted — depending on how you see it — reprehensibly over the sinking of the Belgrano. It took a campaign from Joanna Lumley to give Nepalese Gurkhas the right to live in the United Kingdom and be afforded the rights they were morally, if not legally, entitled to. Politics, politics, and more politics.

Help For Heroes is a charity that focuses on supporting soldiers who are injured during service, and they often enlist the support of public figures and politicians; you may recall the recent furore over Ed Miliband's failure to wear a charity-branded wristband. These are same politicians who do not legislate to properly care for soldiers on their return to the United Kingdom — the Mirror calculated in 2013 that over 9,000 ex-service personnel were homeless — and who have allowed a culture of bullying of many hues to flourish within the institution itself. Politics, politics, and more politics.

We also have a National Armed Forces day in the summer, and representatives from the armed forces are heavily involved in the pre-match rituals of the FA Cup. It is assumed that they will be respectfully applauded as they parade the trophy. John Terry has spoken of his admiration for them, and Wayne Rooney and Joe Hart have been photographed posing with a flag saying, "ARMED FORCES DAY — SHOW YOUR SUPPORT." Despite that, in the past Robbie Fowler was punished by the FA for expressing solidarity with striking dockworkers.

The FA purport to want to keep politics out of football, but in fact they simply want to keep the 'wrong' politics out of football. The armed forces are a tool of British political ambition and responsibility, one over which millions of people have justified concerns, and whatever one thinks of the bravery of the individuals who serve or the nature of the operations they carry out, to argue that they are apolitical is to argue that fish aren't wet. Support for the armed forces — which is, to reiterate, different from respecting Remembrance Sunday — is an explicitly political position, yet it is accepted wholesale by the footballing establishment in a way that virtually no other political position ever could be.

Like many other institutions — newspapers, TV channels, celebrities and politicians — football is increasingly obsessed with becoming the Most Respectful it can be towards the soldiers. This naturally reflects the wider social acceptance for aggressive jingoism, sentimentality and nationalism that puts the army at the centre of society without ever reflecting on what that centrality says, what it represents. It is politics, pure and simple, and it only serves to dilute the genuinely deserved remembrance of those who died in World Wars One and Two. In the rush to be seen to be doing the right thing, football is reflecting the rest of the world; in the rush to honour the Glorious Dead, football is unthinkingly embracing the significantly more inglorious present.[1]

1 This was one of several chapters were just too damn controversial to be published by the Mirror. How did we stick it to the man in response? By meekly accepting the decision that cost us a full £50, and putting it up on Tumblr.

NOVEMBER 8th

Liverpool 1-2 Chelsea

Burnley 1-0 Hull

Manchester United 1-0 Crystal Palace

Southampton 2-0 Leicester

West Ham 0-0 Aston Villa

QPR 2-2 Manchester City

NOVEMBER 9th

Sunderland 1-1 Everton

Tottenham 1-2 Stoke

West Bromwich 0-2 Newcastle

Swansea 2-1 Arsenal

Jose Mourinho, as you may have heard, loves a mind game. He loves a mind game so much that everything he does is a mind game. His choice of clothes is calculated to discombobulate the opposing manager, his stubble length carefully calibrated to inspire just the right amount of masculine inadequacy. He takes exactly three sugars in his tea, because Arsene Wenger takes two.

And if everything that Jose Mourinho does is a mind game, then it follows that everything everyone else does is in response to those mind games. Perhaps Brendan Rodgers might think that his problems this season have been caused by the departure of Luis Suarez, the injuries to Daniel Sturridge, the unsuccessful reinvention of Steven Gerrard as a defensive midfielder and the persistent mediocrity of the defence. What he doesn't know is that each of those can be traced back to a chance meeting with Mourinho over the summer, and a handshake. Chelsea's manager held his hand for just a moment longer than usual, and squeezed just a little firmer than might be considered traditional; Rodgers has been a mess of self-doubt ever since.

Or take Manchester City. Again, you might ascribe their shaky form to the slow adaptation of Eliaquim Mangala and Fernando to English football, the unfortunate absence of David Silva, the dipping form and relevance of Yaya Toure, and a certain tactical inflexibility on the part of their coach. But we can exclusively reveal that Pellegrini's bad mood can be traced back to a box of chocolates sent over by Mourinho as a 'well done on the title gift'. They were mostly delicious, but Pellegrini — who does not read the instructions

— nearly ended up eating a lump of Turkish Delight[1], a confectionery to which he is violently allergic.

Only his wife's quick intervention saved him, and ever since then he's been plagued by questions. Was this simply a thoughtless slip? Did Jose even know about the allergy? Or has the Chelsea manager accrued information about his chocolate eating habits, in an attempt to have him bumped off?

Look at the mess of the Premier League table, and Mourinho's fingerprints are everywhere. Unsolicited restaurant recommendations have been distracting Mauro Pochettino, while a particularly knotty game of postal chess has been keeping Louis van Gaal awake at night. Alan Pardew's only just recovered from a half-friendly, half-aggressive back pat that Mourinho handed out last Christmas. And then, of course, there's Wenger.

After Sunday's meek surrender against Swansea City, Wenger washed his hands of the title race, conceding that Chelsea just look better than everybody else. He looked and sounded as broken as his team; evidence, here, of just how deep under his skin Mourinho has gotten. But where Mourinho has been carefully and scientifically scheming to undermine everybody else, when it comes to Wenger, he hasn't needed to do anything.

When it comes to Wenger, he doesn't need to pull any strings. They pull themselves. His trickery has ascended to a new level: where once he needed to perform the mind games, now he is a mind game, in human form. No chocolates, no chess. Just the simple fact of Mourinho's existence — alive, lurking, up to *something* ... — is enough to knock the Frenchman for a loop. Well, that, and the creeping terror that Chelsea might, just might, go all season unbeaten with a couple fewer draws. It's not possible, says Mourinho, but does he mean it? Is he bluffing? Why would be bluffing? Three sugars, was it?

***

Of course, the other explanation for everybody else being rubbish is that, well, everybody else is a bit rubbish. Manchester United's search for balance is manifesting itself in either too much attack, or too little; on average that might be balance, but on the pitch it's looking weak. City are a one-man team, and so are Arsenal; Liverpool and Tottenham don't even have that luxury. Southampton, meanwhile,

1 Is it "Turkish Delight"? or "Turkish delight"? We didn't care enough to check.

were clever to realise that selling Dejan Lovren would help their defence, but have been skating on the thin ice of a favourable fixture list and a convenient lack of injuries, and will soon find themselves plunged into the inky depths of mediocrity[2].

West Ham and Swansea are fun, and Big Sam is fun and Garry Monk is scary, but neither will last, for existence is a bleak march towards eventual nothingness. Three of the bottom four are getting relegated, the four teams above them aren't even going to have that excitement in their lives, and in a couple of weeks Everton, Stoke, and Newcastle[3] will be able to put their feet up. Chelsea will win the league at a trot, taking as many of the cups as they can be bothered with. Not even the middle of November, and already the January transfer window is looking like the most exciting part of the season. Look what you've done, Jose. You've broken football.

2 This, and many other predictions, show we're better at sniping from the sidelines than attempting to be clever about actual football. Inky mediocrity is a good description for some of our work, though, particularly the sentence you're reading right now.

3 Ahem.

NOVEMBER 15th

England 3-1 Slovenia

NOVEMBER 18th

Scotland 1-3 England

Wayne Rooney, contrary to what a great deal of people think, is not a stupid man. He is not the archetypal chicken-brained buffoon that snobs and the unimaginative assume him to be. Rooney, again contrary to what many people think, is not a bad man. He is not motivated solely by venality, he is not the archetypal spendthrift. He is not even an especially arrogant man, which is rare for men in general, and particularly rare for men who have to believe themselves to be the best in order to maintain a career at the top level.

In interviews he can occasionally reveal himself to be perceptive about his career and where it is headed, and certainly funny — which is an underrated gauge of intelligence[1]. There is also the sense that as he has matured in the last couple of years, perhaps since Alex Ferguson's final season. Or maybe since he tried and failed to force his way out of United to City, he has focussed not on the team (for which he was so useful for for years) but on his own career. By doing so, he may have actually hastened his own decline.

When Rooney started his career with Everton at 16, and for the first few years for England and Manchester United, he was incredible. That is not exaggeration — he could play in a way that was hard to believe an Englishman was doing. His control, pace and creativity came in a mixture that was rarely served anywhere but abroad. The closest comparison was with Paul Gascoigne, and while he is

1 Open goal, there.

thankfully not as prone to self-destruction, he has still proven to be his own worst enemy. Well, either himself or Alex Ferguson.

For a time, he looked like he had the ability be not just Cristiano Ronaldo's equal, but his better. Now, Ronaldo has obviously and comprehensively outstripped Rooney, through hard work as well as talent. He became faster, stronger, more aware and more obsessed with self-improvement; he has honed himself as close to perfection as any athlete in the world. Rooney, while he served the team, never appeared to obsessed with improving his lot. Like a child genius, he seemed to expect that things would always be easy for him. When his body began to fail, or his form stuttered, he did not have hours of application to rival Ronaldo's to fall back on. He had cigarettes and the Stereophonics.

On the pitch, he was moved from Ronaldo's assistant to the centre stage, but at that point, he was no longer a magician. He was briefly an exceptionally effective striker, and linked up with Antonio Valencia and others to an extent that kept the titles coming, and even managed to get into another Champions League final. That final was one that highlighted Ferguson's and the Glazers' failings more than any players, and it is understandable that Rooney was no longer enamoured with the prospect of finishing his career at Old Trafford. Whether he joins another club or not, in one sense he might already have done that, though.

As he has become older, he has become less flexible, physically and tactically. He has lost his physicality, both in terms of being hardy and also with his explosive pace. Injuries weigh him down conspicuously as he cannot rely on the restorative powers of youth. His first touch and passing have been mislaid. Only his goals remain, and they are boosted by his penalty taking. And yet he is first choice, for club and country, with the consensus being that he is a very good player. He is not. He is not even, right now, very good at scoring, his saving grace. As Daniel Harris put it months ago, he went from a fantasy player to a fantasy league player. Now he is not even that, scoring and providing assists rarely this season.

And that has come with another move. He announced that he was now a number 10, and would be 'more intelligent' with his running, meaning he would be covering less ground (remember, his workrate was perhaps his saving grace as his talents left him). He did this at a time that Radamel Falcao had joined and after Robin van Persie had scored that ridiculous goal against Spain for Louis van Gaal's Holland. A cynic would say he had identified he was no longer the main man, and correctly identified that Juan Mata was the most vulnerable. Duly, he began to occupy the number 10 role, and has so far largely been a disaster. When he was sent off against West Ham, it started an undefeated streak for Manchester United. A cynic would note that, upon his return, they lost to a misfiring City.

At United, Rooney was eclipsed by Ronaldo, then by the sense of his own mortality, and realisation that his talents are human. Unlike most players, he did not enter his peak in his later years, and that is nobody's fault but his own. But because England are England, and critical faculties are not our strong point, he remains captain and focal point of the national side.

He won his 100th cap and scored the equaliser, and Hodgson said, "He puts all his enthusiasm and passion into that captaincy." United fans will tell you that explains his performances for United this season, but even for England he has been mediocre, slow and ponderous. To look at Rooney in terms of numbers is one way to credit his achievements, but that he has to be reduced to that is an indictment of his wasted talents.

He said last week that he could not be regarded as a true legend until he won something with England. That is not the reason. It is because he realised too late what it requires to be one, and once again he has shifted his perception of reality to avoid facing the truth. Sven-Goran Eriksson, when he left the England job, begged the nation not to "kill" Wayne Rooney, and England didn't. Instead, we got a slow suicide.[2]

2 He scored the winner against Slovenia in June, to help England on their way to qualification to France 2016, thus securing his name in more record books. That he did it in an otherwise typical performance of poor passing and worse control sums him up.

NOVEMBER 22nd

Chelsea 2-0 West Bromwich
Everton 2-1 West Ham
Leicester 0-0 Sunderland
Manchester City 2-1 Swansea
Newcastle 1-0 QPR
Stoke 1-2 Burnley
Arsenal 1-2 Manchester United

NOVEMBER 23rd

Crystal Palace 3-1 Liverpool
Hull 1-2 Tottenham

NOVEMBER 24th

Aston Villa 1-1 Southampton

ONE: Thank you for coming. Gentlemen, we have a problem. The Premier League has broken.
TWO: Who broke it?
ONE: We don't know. We think it was Jose Mourinho. Or possibly Luis Suarez. The former by arriving and being better than everyone else; the latter by being the same but doing the opposite. Either way, it's knackered, and that's a concern.
THREE: Things looked so hopeful last at the end of last season.
FOUR: A title-race that went down to the wire. The magnificent Moyesification of Manchester United. A top seven that all were all charging into the next season with the hope, the expectation, of improving.
ONE: Indeed. We were all set for a truly epic struggle, but the title race is over. Gentlemen, this isn't good enough. Number Two, what's going on at Liverpool?
TWO: Er, well ...
ONE: Look, we need you to be frank here. Nobody's in trouble, but we need to sort this.
TWO: Well. It turns out that a team built almost entirely around letting two quick, excellent forwards do what they do, can't do anything once one breaks and the other leaves. Everything else that was good about Liverpool last season — the space in which Raheem Sterling and Philippe Coutinho had fun, the passing opportunities afforded to Jordan Henderson and Steven Gerrard — came from Suarez and Sturridge.

FIVE: But that doesn't explain losing to a Neil Warnock side.
TWO: Of course. But you also have to consider the state of that transfer window. You saw it against Crystal Palace: early goal, things going well, then the equaliser comes and the team need to steel themselves. At which point Sterling looks around and sees Rickie Lambert, Adam Lallana looks around and sees the ghost of Steven Gerrard, Joe Allen looks around and sees Brendan Rodgers taking him off, and then everybody looks at Dejan Lovren, who promptly falls over. Not only have they been beheaded, but their guts have fallen out.
ONE: Look, it's not a complete disaster. We can easily repackage Liverpool this season as a kind of Icarus thing. They flew so close, then they sold all their wax, then they plummeted into the sea and drowned horribly. D'you think a tragicomic return of Rafa Benitez might work well later on?
TWO: Oh, definitely. We're already looking into it. He's not Mr Popular in Napoli, would you believe?
ONE: Excellent. Okay. We can work with this. Number Three, what's wrong with Manchester City?
THREE: Buggered if I know. They beat Swansea, just about, though it was as unconvincing a home win as you could hope to see. But are they going to defend their title? No: they can't defend, and with David Silva crocked they have precisely one decent attacker.
ONE: So what's the angle?
THREE: I'm thinking two approaches. One, their humiliating exit from the Champions League is going to make everything spicy, which we can hopefully spin out into some kind of they-spent-how-much-and-this-is-what-they-got-how's-Pep-Guardiola-doing nonsense. And secondly, Vincent Kompany's getting increasingly erratic, and soon somebody's going to notice that he's both brilliant and a liability. So that might be fun.
ONE: Okay. It's a bit thin, but perhaps we can make that work. Number Four, what's going on at Arsenal?
FOUR: Thankfully, Number One, I can report that nothing is going wrong at Arsenal. Everything is as it should be. Last season's cup accident — for which I cannot apologise enough, by the way — is looking more and more like an aberration, and normal service has been resumed. To wit: they can't keep goals out at one end, they can't get them in at the other, and the entire stadium is awash with a kind of privileged and frustrated misery, the vivid hum of a congregation who know, on the one hand, that they're among the luckiest football fans in the world, yet feel, on the other, like everything's going wrong

and it's all falling apart and the world hates them and they're being ripped off.[1]

FIVE: That wine-throwing was a lovely a touch.

FOUR: Thank you. Half of them are blaming Arsene Wenger more than is fair, the other half are forgiving him more than is warranted. And Nacho Monreal is still starting at centre-half, and Jack Wilshere is still arguably the most embarrassing human on the planet.

ONE: Well, that's some good news. What about United, Number Five?

FIVE: Louis van Gaal says everything's going to be fine.

ONE: You don't think this "oh no, not another injury" thing might wear a bit thin?

FIVE: Not really. People love watching United make do and mend. The sight of Paddy McNair and Tyler Blackett lining up alongside Angel di Maria is never not going to be funny. Plus, on a personal level, I'd quite like a crack at the record.

FOUR: At Arsenal's record? At my record?

ONE: Gentlemen, please. Keep things civil.

SIX: Er, if I can just interject here. Chelsea are suffocatingly good.

ONE: We know, Number Six. We know. We're all choked up for you.

SIX: Just thought I should make that clear.

ONE: Now, I've got apologies from Seven and Eight here, but they've been good enough to send me some notes. On Everton, it turns out that they're playing pretty, defensively vulnerable football again, only more so. And on Tottenham, well, the note from Nine just reads: "AVB, AVB, why hast thou forsaken me?" Didn't they get a late winner?

FOUR: Yes, but they were still rubbish. And Harry Kane is still a thing.

ONE: Oh. Oh dear.

[awkward silence]

ONE: Okay, gentlemen. Thank you for your candour, it's hugely appreciated. And let me, too, be candid: this paints a bleak picture. When the comical faceplant of Brendan Rodgers is the most compelling story that the sharp end of a league has to offer, then that league is in trouble. Man cannot live on hubris alone, despite what the Diarists insist. How are we to solve this?

1 They won the FA Cup, but we simply could not find the will to write about it the Monday after it happened. It's hard to get excited about Arsenal when they have simply moved up one place in the league because Manchester United were so rubbish, rather than because they're any good. Of course, Arsenal fans are convinced they've taken a step up in quality this year, but they all think Tomas Rosicky is excellent because he showboated against Brighton.

FOUR: Deduct points from Chelsea?
ONE: Probably unconstitutional.
THREE: Give points to everybody else?
ONE: Likewise.
TWO: Accept that some years are simply going to be better than others, embrace the cyclical nature of football, recognise that today's champion are tomorrow's clowns, and simply get on with enjoying what we have, which, in the grand scheme of things, is pretty okay?

[awkward silence]

ONE: Don't be ridiculous.
THREE: We could ... rebrand?
ONE: What?
Three: Rebrand. How about: "THE WORST LEAGUE IN THE WORLD"?

[silence]

FOUR: ... I like it. It has punch.
SIX: Yeah. It's ... fresh.
FIVE: It's surprising. Unprecedented. Distinctive. "WATCH THE PREMIER LEAGUE, IT'S CRAP".
SIX: "AS BAD AS IT GETS".
THREE: "STAGNANT SUNDAY".
TWO: If nothing else, it'll get the last few remaining Serie A fans on board.

[silence]

ONE: Splendid. Gentlemen, you are a pleasure to work with. Let's go to work. After lunch.

NOVEMBER 29th

West Bromwich 0-1 Arsenal
Burnley 1-1 Aston Villa
Liverpool 1-0 Stoke
Manchester United 3-0 Hull
QPR 3-2 Leicester
Swansea 1-1 Crystal Palace
West Ham 1-0 Newcastle
Sunderland 0-0 Chelsea

NOVEMBER 30th

Southampton 0-3 Manchester City
Tottenham 2-1 Everton

Following last week's crisis meeting in the Premier League PR bunker, it seemed like nothing had changed. It was still The Worst League In The World ^{TM} and it was as predictable as ever. It was like waking up on a Monday and feeling, at the pit of your stomach, a sense not just of doom, but of a rising panic as you realise not only can you not get out of work today, you can't get out of it for at least another 30 years. Unless, of course, you choose death now, and even if you hang on for another 30 years, death will then be only just around the corner. You're there. Monday's there. You're looking at each other and you know that Monday's won, because there are more Mondays to come than there are excuses you could ever try to give your boss.[1]

With that established, let's have a look at just how predictable it all was at the weekend.

Diego Costa carries on in a relentlessly prickish manner

There's nothing wrong with some straightforward violence and intimidation on a football pitch. Strong tackles, and maybe even a consensual fist fight are both things that can be excused by most sensible people watching a football game. What isn't enjoyable is deliberate elbows into the face, and tackles that deliberately injure or could well injure people. The difference was obvious between Diego

1 We can't recall what put us in such a foul mood that particular morning, but evidently somebody had pissed on our cornflakes and made our cornflakes out of piss as well.

Costa and John O'Shea on Saturday, when O'Shea and Costa both battered each other gamely for much of the match, but Costa whacked a hand into Wes Brown and also tried to put his studs into O'Shea's chest. Still, Diego Costa seems to be the new John Aldridge, and has been for most of the season (except he's much better at football). No change there then.

Michael Carrick plays well against poor side, his advocates go over the top

Hull are out of form, and Hatem Ben Arfa was so out of form that Steve Bruce removed him from the game against Manchester United in the first half, not due to injury. As is tradition, Bruce knew exactly how to line up against United — just as he does every time. Sitting back, no ambition, waiting for defeat and death. And so it proved, 3-0, absolutely easy for United. Carrick was given more room than he had been for years and was able to show off his passing range. He didn't have to track runners, not that he ever bothers to do that anymore.

As a result, it gave people the chance to decry his absence from the England side, that if he had been born in another country he'd be more appreciated, and using the same phrases as ever — the quarterback role, spraying passes around, a metronome. Particularly metronome, which needs to be taken out and shot. "Let's get out there and play all our football at exactly the same speed, lads! Predictable tempo! Nobody rush anywhere!" Football isn't a game for metronomes, it's a game for jazz trumpeters, solo violinists, timpani and the occasional bassoon.

All words that when employed in football should result in an instant journalistic P45. Still, the same as it ever was.

Arsene Wenger defends his legacy

Another bright spot as Arsenal show their true strength to stay in touch with the top four until they mount their late charge to the Champions League spaces. They might have lost in the most cowardly fashion to Manchester United in their last game. They might have lost players to injury, twice to the same position against West Brom, and earlier to Jack Wilshere suffering the consequences of being A Famous England Player Who Cannot Be Sent Off. After this week's game Wenger defended himself as a pocket of Arsenal fans expressed frustration with the limited ambition he shows every week and every season, saying:

"Look, in the last 15 years we are qualified for the last 16 in the Champions League. Give me another club who has done that," Wenger said. "I think we have shown extreme consistency and that's all we can do. We've had ups and downs in the league — yes, it's true, but you only come back again when the spirit is strong and healthy and united inside the club. And I think if you have shown such a consistency it's because we have that at the club. We have values and we respect them."

He perfectly encapsulated everything some Arsenal fans dislike about him, and everything every other fan mocks him for. Same old, same old ...

... wait, Joe Cole scored a goal, Glen Johnson scored a goal, Simon Mignolet saved a shot, Roberto Soldado scored a goal, Spurs beat a side with 11 men, Chris Smalling scored a goal, and Chelsea drew ...

... sorry, what? Something new! Screw you, boss, I'm not coming in!

DECEMBER 2nd

Burnley 1-1 Newcastle
Leicester 1-3 Liverpool
Manchester United 2-1 Stoke
Swansea 2-0 QPR
Crystal Palace 0-1 Aston Villa
West Bromwich 1-2 West Ham

DECEMBER 3rd

Arsenal 1-0 Southampton
Chelsea 3-0 Tottenham
Everton 1-1 Hull
Sunderland 1-4 Manchester City

DECEMBER 6th

Newcastle 2-1 Chelsea
Hull 0-0 West Bromwich
Liverpool 0-0 Sunderland
QPR 2-0 Burnley
Stoke 3-2 Arsenal
Tottenham 0-0 Crystal Palace
Manchester City 1-0 Everton

DECEMBER 7th

West Ham 3-1 Swansea
Aston Villa 2-1 Leicester

DECEMBER 8th

Southampton 1-2 Manchester United

It's been an inconvenient weekend for Diarists, dear readers. Like you, we spent all week reading article after article on the ascent of Chelsea to the very tip of the pantheon. Better than anything Alex Ferguson had cobbled together? Destined to make the Arsenal Invincibles look like thoroughly vincible charlatans? A sort of cross between Ajax '95, Real Madrid '60, and the X-Men? Yep, yep and yep yep yep. So convinced were we by this case that we actually wrote the Diary on Friday afternoon, praising Mourinho's men for another step along the road to immortality that they'd already completed, then spent our weekends lounging at increasingly unlikely angles in increasingly disreputable bars.

So it was something of a surprise to find out, come Monday morning and the clearing of the fog, that they'd lost at Newcastle and we had to delete everything. (Oh, the jokes you've missed out on.) Naturally we assumed something utterly incomprehensible had happened. Maybe Diego Costa had taken exception to the Angel of the North's provocative 'come on then' stance and attempted to headbutt 200 tonnes of steel to the ground, or the cosiness of black and white on the opposing kits had driven John Terry to outraged confusion. Imagine our surprise, then, to find out that something even stranger had happened:

Chelsea had lost a game of football that was just a game of football.

Obviously, Jose Mourinho tried his best to inject some kind of silliness into the post-game fallout. Ballboys on the one hand — "it is not possible to play with two balls ..." — and metaphorical ambling cows on the other. "You may as well put a cow in the middle of the pitch, walking. And then stop the game because there was a cow." But even he couldn't disguise what had happened. A decent, entertaining game of football had resulted in a slightly surprising result. It was, for everybody involved, deeply embarrassing.

This is not what the Premier League is about! Its big sides don't lose to its littler sides like this, in humdrum, banal fashion! They lose because of Uefa conspiracies; because of refereeing incompetence; because of grand conjunctions of malignant astral forces. Not because their second choice defensive midfielder isn't very good and their attackers had a bit of a collective off day. Not because Newcastle defended with admirable stoicism and a touch of fortune. This is not the way of the best league in the world! Quick, somebody set fire to something.

There is, of course, one consequence of all this premature acclamation. Chelsea are still going to win the title, likely by an obscene margin, and yet in comparison to the Chelsea That Swallows The Universe, the imaginary Chelsea that never existed, they're only ever going to be a slight disappointment. Essentially, we've ruined them for ourselves. Were we really all that desperate for Mourinho to get another one, the ultimate one (No, not that. Grow up.) over Arsene Wenger?

***

Well, of course we were. While Wenger seems like a decent man[1], the curiosity of a football club he's helped to create is such a volatile thing — an institution at once achingly superior yet astoundingly brittle — that it's almost impossible not to want them to cock up every week or so, just to see what happens. Who else but Arsenal could begin a football match buoyed by the knowledge that their greatest recent achievement was safe for another year, yet end it with their own fans booing their manager on the platform of Stoke-on-Trent train station?

1 Who, with his heavy financial involvement in the club has priced out much of the local community, and in a diverse borough of London, tried to sign the definitely-not-racist Luis Suarez, and who trades in teenage kids from abroad at a discount while complaining about financial doping. But decent by football standards.

***

We're not going to dwell on Arsenal, because the definition of insanity is repeating the definition of insanity over and over again while Calum Chambers[2] tries not to get booked, again. We will simply note that while booing in a crowd is, if not acceptable, than at least part of a mass expression and so understandable in its lack of nuance. Whereas booing on a train platform really drives home the fact that a grown man making the noise "boo" is arguably the least dignified thing that a grown man can do. Except, perhaps, shout "Get out while you can, Joel!" at a footballer[3]. He's not been kidnapped, you buffoon.

Instead, we're going to talk about the majesty of Andy Carroll and the wonder that is Big Sam Allardyce. At the time of writing, West Ham are the third best team in the country, a sentence that doesn't get any less ridiculous the longer you look at it. But while their early season success was predicated on exciting, unpredictable attacking football, the return to fitness of Carroll has enabled him to return to what he truly loves. A big man. A Big Man.

Goal the first: a remarkable header from a decent cross. Goal the second: a slightly less remarkable but still rather competent header from an equally acceptable cross. The only surprise was that Allardyce didn't greet the third goal — a long punt down the middle, a nod on from the big man, a spanking finish from the little man — by tearing off his clothes, standing tumescent and resplendent in the middle of the Upton Park pitch, and bellowing "ARE YOU NOT ENTERTAINED?" at the assembled faithful.

We can think of no more fitting man to occupy the Olympic Stadium than this shining example of everything that is absolutely British about Britain: reductive football, overweening self-belief, and an instinctive distrust of, well, almost everything else. This is Carroll. See him jump. This is Allardyce. Hear him roar. Watch out, penalty areas and soft cheekbones of Europe. Big Sam's a-coming.[4]

2 One 'L'. Who does he think he is? This footnote brought to you by the half of the book that doesn't spell his name with an "i" like a pillock.

3 Joel Campbell got out though. Nice to see footballers listening to their fans for once.

4 Big Sam is not a-coming, because the arse fell out of the season as it became clear he and the owners would be parting ways by mutual contempt.

DECEMBER 13th

Burnley 1-0 Southampton
Chelsea 2-0 Hull
Crystal Palace 1-1 Stoke
Leicester 0-1 Manchester City
Sunderland 1-1 West Ham
West Bromwich 1-0 Aston Villa
Arsenal 4-1 Newcastle

DECEMBER 14th

Manchester United 3-0 Liverpool
Swansea 1-2 Tottenham

DECEMBER 15th

Everton 3-1 QPR

Brendan Rodgers woke up with his head resting on his personalised, ergonomic pillow, with his sheets made from the finest Egyptian cotton. The sheets had over 800 thread count, but Brendan was still looking for a higher count, knowing that he needed to treat himself as well as possible, to be at the top of his game.

He reached over to stick on the Nespresso machine, and put in a bespoke cartridge, with the finest bean blend he felt he could design. He felt like he'd missed out on a gap year to Africa when he was a professional footballer, so in the summer he'd visited Ethiopia. He thought back to the summer, when he was teaching the coffee farms how best to manage their staff, and just how grateful they'd been when he'd left at the end of his visit, no doubt because of all the inspiring messages he'd given to them. The coffee, to him, tasted of a time when he had helped those who were not quite as excellent at achieving excellence at he was, and he felt that was an important metaphor for the day's team talk.

He flicked on his customised iPad, with a Latin inscription of 'You'll Never Walk Alone' lasered onto the back of the tablet, and made a note of it for later. He then reached across into his bedside table drawer, and took out a Moleskin notebook, and also wrote — in Mont Blanc ballpoint — the same note. He was aware that he wanted to make the job as easy as possible when it came to whoever edited his diaries, and didn't want to risk losing all his aphorisms and tactical observations through a virus or technical mishap. He also looked up each word in Spanish on Google Translate, and made another copy for those abroad who followed his work. Although he was fluent, obviously, he didn't want to take chances. He knew that he had to respect his fans as much as they clearly respected — some might say admired — him. He made his way to his chrome-laden en suite bathroom.

Brendan lived in the Liver Gardens Buildings in Cheshire. He said to himself: "My name is Brendan Rodgers. I'm 41 years old. I believe in taking care of myself, and a balanced diet and a rigorous exercise routine. In the morning, if my face is a little puffy, I'll put on an ice pack while doing my stomach crunches. I can do a thousand now. After I remove the ice pack I use a deep pore cleanser lotion. In the shower I use a water activated gel cleanser, then a honey almond body scrub, and on the face an exfoliating gel scrub. Then I apply an herb-mint facial masque which I leave on for 10 minutes while I prepare the rest of my routine. I always use an after shave lotion with little or no alcohol, because alcohol dries your face out and makes you look older. Then moisturiser, then an anti-ageing eye balm followed by a final moisturising protective lotion. There is an idea of a Brendan Rodgers. Some kind of inspiration. And though I can try to hide my determined, forceful gaze, and you can shake my hand and feel flesh gripping yours, and maybe you can even sense our lifestyles are probably comparable, I simply am achieving excellence on a scale not comparable to you."

His morning routine left him ready for the day. He knew that he was performing at a level not since, well, he couldn't think of someone that was a bigger inspiration to himself than he was, and he smiled at just how well he was doing, and how well he knew himself.

Dressed in an Armani suit that had been altered for his newly muscular frame, and wearing the Hugo Boss sunglasses he needed to dull the sight of his teeth in his car mirror, he drove to meet the players. He knew it was all about appearances, about confidence, about showing his players that he was a leader of men. He knew that Mario was part of his family now, but it required something special, something that only he could imagine to win against Manchester United.

He got on the team coach. He spread his arms out to either side of him, a kind of Jesus pose[1]. The players knew that was the sign for silence and looked towards him, and they waited for him to speak. Brendan felt their gaze, and he knew he was home. He knew this was

1 He'd taken the classic messianic position and added his own little improvements.

crucial, that what he said next would define the next three hours, and he wasn't going to get it wrong. He knew it had to be simple and that the metaphor he'd noted earlier wasn't quite right, and he would save it for Wembley in May. He brought his hands in a praying motion, just in front of his mouth and smirked.

He looked every player in the eye and then said:

"Three at the back. Jones in for Mignolet. Sterling a false nine. You're welcome."

He sat down, and looked out of the window at the sun in the sky. He was Brendan, and he liked it.[2]

2 Weirdly, this was the second blog that wasn't run. Parody is very rarely libellous, but it's a sensible choice not to provoke such an important institution in the media as Liverpool Football Club Football Club.

DECEMBER 20th

Manchester City 3-0 Crystal Palace
Aston Villa 1-1 Manchester United
Hull 0-1 Swansea
QPR 3-2 West Bromwich
Southampton 3-0 Everton
Tottenham 2-1 Burnley
West Ham 2-0 Leicester

DECEMBER 21st

Newcastle 0-1 Sunderland
Liverpool 2-2 Arsenal

DECEMBER 22nd

Stoke 0-2 Chelsea

Super Sunday is generally an exaggeration, and occasionally an outright lie, but sometimes it lives up to its own hysterical billing. With the appetite whetted by Sunderland's profoundly amusing win at Newcastle — the footballing equivalent of creeping up behind Alan Pardew and flicking his ear really hard — the stage was set for an absolute cracker at Anfield. What more could anybody ask for? Two teams, and two managers, both utterly determined to do whatever it took to lose the game.

Arsenal made the stronger start, Arsene Wenger cleverly setting his side up to isolate his most potent attacking players while simultaneously leaving the hilariously sub-standard Mathieu Flamini exposed in front of the defence. Flamini played his part to perfection, picking up a silly yellow card and then a final warning in quick succession. And though Wenger would doubtless have liked to concede the two or three that Arsenal's first-half performance deserved, he would nevertheless have been satisfied with the deficit his side were taking in at half time. Advantage north London …

… well, nearly. If we've learned one thing about Liverpool this season, it's never underestimate their ability to snatch parity from the jaws of a lead. Over went Alexis Sanchez, in went the free kick, and up to no avail went one, two, three defenders. There is a stroke of artistic genius in permitting Arsenal to equalise thanks to headers won in the penalty area by diminutive Frenchmen: a simultaneous bird-flip to everybody in the stadium, whether they've come to see Arsenal's pretty triangles or to see Martin Skrtel hd th bll vgrsly. More on that later.

So, Rodgers' momentary masterstroke cancelled out Wenger's slick longer game, and the race for the zero points was level after 45 minutes. Into the second half, and Liverpool started the stronger: okay, so Raheem Sterling kept undermining his team's best efforts by running at people, then past people, but at the other end, just after the hour mark, Skrtel and friends pounced. Leaving one Arsenal player in space might have been an accidental. Leaving all of them in space? Magisterial stuff.

Arsenal, sensing that things were starting to get away from them, began to drop deeper and deeper, almost begging Liverpool to equalise. But Liverpool held firm and left Arsenal's net untroubled, before Brendan Rodgers pulled what should have been the decisive masterstroke. On went Fabio Borini, with strict instructions to 'play like a hyperactive manchild and see what happens'. Off came Fabio Borini, having taken that to mean 'throw the ball away after failing to win a throw-in before kicking Santi Cazorla in the tit'. 2-1 down, one man down: the loss was Liverpool's.

Or it should have been. But if we've learned one thing about Arsenal, it's that they never give up their restless pursuit of failing to win games of football. Much has been made of the strengths and weaknesses of zonal marking, as opposed to man-to-man, and credit needs to be given to Wenger. Because when it comes to conceding those 97th minute equalisers, nothing beats good, solid, old-fashioned bad marking. Turns out that when Martin Skrtel is free from terrifying presence of Mathieu Debuchy, he's quite good at jumping. Bonus points for having the biggest defender on the pitch cringe out of the way like a man suddenly taken aback by a violent sneeze.[1] Everybody saw, Per Mertesacker. Everybody saw.

1 As we read this back we've noticed 90% of the book is criticising Arsenal in a year they finished third and won the FA Cup. They can end this by finishing second or first next year, which is to say they won't and can't end this.

DECEMBER 26th

Chelsea 2-0 West Ham
Crystal Palace 1-3 Southampton
Burnley 0-1 Liverpool
Manchester United 3-1 Newcastle
Everton 0-1 Stoke
Sunderland 1-3 Hull
West Bromwich 1-3 Manchester City
Leicester 1-2 Tottenham
Swansea 1-0 Aston Villa
Arsenal 2-1 QPR

DECEMBER 28th

Tottenham 0-0 Manchester United
Southampton 1-1 Chelsea
Stoke 2-0 West Bromwich
West Ham 1-2 Arsenal
Aston Villa 0-0 Sunderland
Hull 0-1 Leicester
Manchester City 2-2 Burnley
QPR 0-0 Crystal Palace
Newcastle 3-2 Everton

DECEMBER 29th

Liverpool 4-1 Swansea

In 2010, Narrative was quietly minding its business, happily meaning an account of a sequence of events, or a story. Narrative had never been exploited by anyone, and had never gone out of its way to pester anyone in return. It was just getting by, doing its job. Clocking in and clocking out. Median man, no time for causing trouble. That was before the politicians got involved. Then Narrative was called in for overtime, and asked to do things that it had never really done before. It was asked not just to mean a statement, a rehearsal or used in fiction to describe from whose point of view things were being said. It was now asked to do things without being qualified, and had to mean things like a recurrent motif or theme, and like Trope it was bullied into appearing everywhere.

Narrative and Trope looked at each other, appalled, wondering what happened to their past lives, ones that everyone had seemed satisfied for. But now they were there, joined by Disconnect. Abused, beaten and kicked around for people who couldn't write and had to latch on to oddly academic but unclear terminology in order to set themselves apart. They were now the lackeys of the political set, and language was being destroyed.

And while Trope and Disconnect were always with Narrative in Guardian thinkpieces and politicians' answers on Radio 4 today, Narrative was being worked ever harder, as the football media stepped in, determined to make him one of their own, too. Now it wasn't just that he had to mean all kinds of obfuscating nonsense at the behest of red-tie wearing Boden humanoids bent on destroying societal institutions at various paces, now he had to lazily be attached to cliches that everybody with a passing interest in football had identified.

Narrative was used by tactics and analytics bods to decry normal people who enjoyed football beyond the numbers, and was used as a way of saying that it was human nature to ascribe meaning to things associated with victories in football, like the "down to 10 men Narrative" or the "curse of the ex-Narrative." Narrative was knackerd and overused, but it didn't stop there. Narrative was for the sideways glance, too.

People would tell us all about the Narrative of Jose Mourinho and Sam Allardyce as joyless brutes being incorrect. They would say that the Narrative of Liverpool's charge for the title in 2013/14 was the Narrative that defined the season, and that there were Narratives within Narratives, as the Hillsborough anniversary and Steven Gerrard's desire for the Premier League and Luis Suarez's redemption Narrative piled up into one enormo-Narrative that sent Narrative to the computer, searching for rehab for mental exhaustion after Narrative had so many personalities and traits that he was no longer sure whether he really was a Narrative anymore, and whether or not what he was doing and saying was a Narrative anymore, and then he started saying that his own Narrative was one of a meta-Narrative forcing him in on himself, the Narrative of sudden fame causing a nervous breakdown.

And still it didn't stop. The World Cup came, and the Narrative of the homecoming of football to Brazil exhausted him over the summer. You could not move for Narrative being called to come in and perform. The Narrative of Steven Gerrard's decline extending against Luis Suarez, his team-mate at Liverpool, and the Narrative of yet another Suarez moment of self-sabotage, and the Narrative of Uruguayans protecting their own. The Narrative of Spurs then assaulted Liverpool, who had spent millions on replacing their own Gareth Bale. Manchester United threw aside their own Narrative of bringing through young players, taking on Radamel Falcao and Angel Di Maria. Arsenal set about continuing their own Narrative as the season went on, falling into the Not Quite Good Enough Narrative.

City continued to struggle, but then asked Narrative to work double time, as the Narrative of the Uninspiring Pellegrini was matched by the Narrative of Famous European victories clashed against each other, and the Narrative of a Title Charge ignored the Narrative of Chelsea walking away with the title.

It got to Boxing Day, and with three games in quick succession on the horizon, Narrative had had enough. “That’s it,” Narrative said. “No more Narratives, no more shocks. Everyone will win who is supposed to, there will be no shocks. Arsenal, Chelsea, Manchester City and United will all win.”

Two days later, Narrative stepped in again, saying, “It’s too much. I can’t conjure up any more of my own Narrative twice in 48 hours, it’s physically and mentally not possible to recover so much. In the first half I could just about produce some acceptable-level Narrative, but in the second half it wasn’t so much about Narrative as much as it was an attempt at survival. Draws for everyone at the top, I can’t handle any more title Narrative now, it’s too much.”

“There will be no more upsets over Christmas. It will be too boring and obvious to invoke me or anything at all. For the love of God, stop using me. Leave me alone and find a new word to bother in 2015. Can’t you talentless hacks find another word to bother?”

JANUARY 1st

Stoke 1-1 Manchester United
Hull 2-0 Everton
Manchester City 3-2 Sunderland
QPR 1-1 Swansea
Southampton 2-0 Arsenal
West Ham 1-1 West Bromwich
Aston Villa 0-0 Crystal Palace
Liverpool 2-2 Leicester
Newcastle 3-3 Burnley
Tottenham 5-3 Chelsea

Jose Mourinho checked the windows. The tape was secure, the fabric thick and black. Not a chink of light was getting through; he was safe from prying eyes, from long lenses, from powerful telescopes.

Nobody's seeing in here.

He pulled a chair over and began to check the ceiling. The tinfoil was peeling in places, so he spent half an hour or so applying more of the glue and smoothing out the edges. He had been weighing up the practicality of putting a fourth layer on for a while now, but the events of the last few weeks had made up his mind. He simply couldn't afford to take chances.

Nothing's getting in that way.

The next step, as always, was to inventory his supplies. Mineral water. Shotgun cartridges. Hammer. Axe[1]. The task usually soothed him, but today he was too agitated, too distracted. His mind was racing.

What are they up to? What do they know?

---

1 Probably could have put some comedy football ones in here. "Solar-charged Jon Obi Mikel," that kind of thing. Still, too late now.

Images began to pop into his mind, unbidden. Cesc Fabregas, lying in the penalty are, blood spurting from his severed foot. The referee: laughing. Eden Hazard, fighting to escape Fazio's brutal chokehold. The referee: forty yards away, facing the wrong direction. Gary Cahill, Oscar, Branislav Ivanovic, saving their careers and their limbs by leaping out of the way of actual, literal scythes. The referee: taking names, cackling. Jan Vertonghen, holding the ball, stroking it, tossing it lightly from hand to hand. The referee: absent, uncaring, elsewhere.

Even Eden said it wasn't a foul. Have they got to him too?

And the press! Oh, the press! Of course, they pretended that they were praising his boys, with their talk of invincibility, of toppling Arsenal from their gilded perch. It looked like they were just getting carried away with themselves. But he knew what they were up to. How to keep his charges hungry when they've already been proclaimed the greatest side in the world? How to keep focused when the thought — the delicious thought — of cheapening Arsene Wenger's greatest achievement was everywhere.

Stay focused, I said. They didn't. They couldn't.

He looked at his phone. Unlisted, temporary; he changed handsets every twelve hours as a matter of course. Only Roman and big JT knew how to contact him here. And yet, there on the screen, a blinking icon. A message.

How did they get my number?

Had he recently been involved in a no-fault accident?
He laughed, bitterly.

If they only knew.

Too distracted to complete his tallies, he opened his laptop. After engaging the usual plethora of IP maskers, anonymisers, and so on and so forth, he was safely online. News of Steven Gerrard's departure from Liverpool raised a wry smile — he would, of course, have come to Chelsea had the Queen not asked MI5 to intervene — until he realised that the months of saturation coverage would only distract attention from the machinations against his team. He felt physically sick. Not even a few minutes spent commenting on Rafa Benitez's blog could cheer him up.

How to bring the injustices of the world to light, in a nation fawning over a man who never even won the league?

His scowl deepened when he saw footage of Gary Cahill's selfless intervention to save Harry Kane's life being described as a "kick", a "stamp", and a "disgrace". Naturally, all the footage had been tampered with. The highly dangerous spiders had been carefully airbrushed from the scene, and nobody was mentioning the thank you note Kane had dropped round after the game.

They're going to ban him. They're going to ban him.

Jose sat very still, his mind whirling at the scale of the campaign against him. He counted to ten, carefully, mastering his rage, schooling his anger. He would beat them, he promised himself. He would beat them all. He was just one man, but he was one man fighting with the truth on his side, and the truth can never be defeated. He could do this. He could overcome them all. His Chelsea, his boys. They'd be fine.

Might check the curtains again.[2]

2 At the end of the season Jose Mourinho admitted he'd gone a bit far with the conspiracy stuff, but will it change next season? Will it fuck. And neither will the determination of the press to take everything he says at face value.

JANUARY 3rd

Leicester City 1-0 Newcastle United
Tranmere Rovers 2-6 Swansea City
West Bromwich Albion 7-0 Gateshead
Barnsley 0-2 Middlesbrough

JANUARY 4th

Dover Athletic 0-4 Crystal Palace
Queens Park Rangers 0-3 Sheffield United
Sunderland 1-0 Leeds United
Aston Villa 1-0 Blackpool
Manchester City 2-1 Sheffield Wednesday
Southampton 1-1 Ipswich Town
Stoke City 3-1 Wrexham
Yeovil Town 0-2 Manchester United
Chelsea 3-0 Watford
Arsenal 2-0 Hull City

JANUARY 5th

Burnley 1-1 Tottenham Hotspur
AFC Wimbledon 1-2 Liverpool

JANUARY 6th

Everton 1-1 West Ham United

With the relative lack of excitement from the FA Cup, with few engaging upsets and weakened teams from many of the Premier League sides, it was shaping up to be a fairly dull weekend.

That, sadly, was until Oldham Athletic's executives decided to act on the behalf of their manager and fans, and put their hands into a toaster, flick the switch, and jump into a swimming pool with it.

If doing the same thing again and again and expecting different results is the definition of insanity, then trying to employ Ched Evans again and again and thinking the reaction of the public will be different is the definition of owning a lower league football club.

It feels similarly repetitive to have to state the case against Evans being employed for yet another time, but also necessary, such is the sheer scale of the unpleasant, wilfully damaging and dangerous attitude of some in the game. Not all by any means — many supporters and staff of clubs are disgusted by him — but enough that it will only go further to make life worse for women generally, and Ched Evans' victim specifically.

Ched Evans is often painted sympathetically as a victim by cherry-picking, distorting and occasionally just flat-out misrepresenting aspects of the case that might hint at his innocence, while ignoring the wider weight of evidence that led a jury to convict him, a conviction that has already been upheld on appeal. (A review is pending.)

The most craven of all articles do not vouch for his innocence, but rather claim things like, "there are no winners here," in order to draw some kind of false equivalence between the suffering of both of the parties, Evans and his victim. They have indeed both suffered, but as a result of the actions of just one man — Evans himself.

Before we come to the crime itself, it's worth taking a look at Evans' actions since his release.

While his subsequent apology — to his girlfriend, and only to his girlfriend, and only for "infidelity" — might have been limited by his desire to maintain his innocence with a review pending, he has taken no public steps to stop his friends and family from campaigning on his behalf with a website that has encouraged — by design or not — the harassment of his victim.

Given that his victim has had to change her identity and address five times, and was unable to spend Christmas with her family for fear of harassment, it appears that his supporters have taken to ruining her life as a pastime.

Evans has at no point publicly asked his supporters to stop ruining this woman's life; given that he must surely know it is happening, we can only assume he tacitly condones the actions. Imagine the dead-eyed hatred of a man who would not step in at this point, even out of a sense of protecting what scraps of a reputation he has left.

On a wider scale of depressing behaviour, consider the actions of fans who use him as a tool to generally intimidate women, and stroll around in packs wearing Ched Evans masks, or sing that Ched Evans will "do what he wants."

"Women of Bradford, he's coming for you," as at least one train carriage of football fans has recently had it; a rape threat doesn't get any less hideous for being to the tune of Sloop John B, and doesn't get any less revolting for apparently being "just banter".

Or have a look at the women online who speak out about Evans' contribution to rape culture. Men, who appear personally offended by the idea that they can no longer sleep with women unable to give consent, treat this as an opportunity to issue sexual abuse and threats across every avenue of online commentary provided.

It is as if thousands of men have realised that they are rapists, or potential rapists, or at best strongly supportive of acts that amount to rape, yet rather than change their actions and beliefs, would like to change the definition of rape in the law so that they can carry on. As if "frankly, as a society, we interpret rape too widely" was any kind of reasonable position. The wider culture can obviously not be laid at Evans' feet, but the impunity they feel to discuss this so openly around his case has been clearly fuelled by his arrogance.

A lot of the time, this is seen as part of a drive to sanitise football. The often-heard refrain is that, "you can't say anything these days," which is then invariably linked to political correctness and the modernisation of football.

Given that there are plenty of accounts that stewards were unwilling to remove people who take part in racist chants, it does seem that you can still say plenty. Given that an ex-player was heard in a press room saying that rape in football was often the fault of the woman, it does seem that you can say plenty more.

If you think that football is being unfairly changed when people seek to challenge others for being sexist, racist or homophobic, then it's not football that has changed to unsettle you, it is the world. If that is how you provoke people, with bigotry, then you are not trying hard enough.

And if Evans is at the centre of all this, partly he is to blame, partly others are to blame for their own actions. Football fans often claim — when it is important to them — that football clubs are part of their community. The ones who object to Evans' excommunication are now handily forgetting that.

Chairmen often use a football club as a way to elevate their standing in their communities, and wax gaseous about their love for the town and community. They too now handily forget that.

A club has a responsibility to its fans and its community, and that responsibility surely extends to avoiding any association with unrepentant, life-destroying rapists. Even if they might score a few goals.

Evans raped a woman, was found to have done so beyond reasonable doubt by a jury, was further found to have done so by an appeal court that rejected his submission. Yet rather than apologise for doing so — which would be the start, not the end, of any attempt to redeem himself — he is spending tens of thousands of pounds on an assault on the legal definition of rape.

Since release, he has taken no public action to prevent a website to spur on people to harass a woman into hiding. He has encouraged clubs to offer him work and try to return to football, to be venerated by rape-defending fans.

Evans has made the world to be a less safe, more aggressive space for women to exist in. He hasn't hurt just one woman, he has hurt many more of them in ways he cannot grasp yet. The clubs who try to hire him do the same. Oldham Athletic have apparently been "surprised" at the strength of feeling against his signing. That, in its own way, is remarkably depressing.

Evans does have a right to return to work. Equally, people have a right to speak out when that work offered is on a public stage, in a position that carries with it a complex weight of public responsibilities.

Because it ultimately isn't a question of rights — which is often invoked when cowardly devil's advocates are too scared to say they don't consider rape to be rape — but a question of what is right and wrong. To consider the law suddenly to be the world's sole moral arbiter is a dangerous road to go down for us all.[1]

1 "But it's legal!" is the most inane justification for an action that the world has come up with. Hollyoaks is legal, and nobody thinks that's right.

JANUARY 10th

Sunderland 0-1 Liverpool
Burnley 2-1 QPR
Chelsea 2-0 Newcastle
Everton 1-1 Manchester City
Leicester 1-0 Aston Villa
Swansea 1-1 West Ham
West Bromwich 1-0 Hull
Crystal Palace 2-1 Tottenham

JANUARY 11th

Arsenal 3-0 Stoke
Manchester United 0-1 Southampton

After the defeat at home to Southampton, the autopsy began on Manchester United. Which was unfortunate, obviously, as there was no chance of actually locating any heart or guts. United had set up with no wit or invention, and while they defended reasonably competently for the first half, they also offered no guile, creativity or pace in attack, just as they hadn't for most of the season. Someone on Twitter asked, "which players does this system get the best out of?" The problem for United is that currently, it's David De Gea.

Another, possibly more telling point was also made, that Manchester United's biggest advantage this season was the relative poverty of the quality of their rivals. Clearly, this referred to Southampton, Liverpool, Arsenal and Spurs, which is damning for United. In most other recent seasons, when they were good, you would consider their main rivals to be Manchester City and Chelsea. You know, the teams that would actually challenge for the league. This, in turn, demonstrates the utter garbage that Louis van Gaal was left to resolve when he took over.[1]

It is hard to escape that the hardcore of United fans who had pointed out that Alex Ferguson had crippled his squad but kept them running on the fumes of his genius have ultimately been proved correct. David Moyes was not cut out to succeed him, and was hamstrung by Edward Woodward, but the collapse from first to seventh showed

1 What an incredible legacy Alex Ferguson, who clearly so loved the club, to leave behind a squad which will conceivably have none of his players in the first team at the start of 2015/16. Except Wayne Rooney, who is half the player he was.

how precarious United's squad was balanced. That meant that in the summer, United might well have spent £150 million, but it appears to be nowhere near enough. With a central defender a priority for this transfer window, it seems like Van Gaal will need to be given at least another year before his work can be accurately judged.

But it's not just the problems with the squad that have held him back. Constant injuries, perhaps a tribute to the fallen in the centenary year of the start of World War One, have stopped Van Gaal from doing little more than carrying out running repairs and making enough of an ever changing, but always depleted squad. Because the side have been held back so long because of this, because Angel Di Maria was finally making a league return from his own injury, because Van Gaal has the goodwill of the crowd, and because £150 million is still objectively a huge amount of money, this game against Southampton was the chance to see the real United. Oh dear.

And in a sense, it was. United have been largely boring since the turn of 2013 and the end of Van Persie's run of form. After then, it was apparent that United struggled to break down organised sides, Wayne Rooney could not control a football (and still can't), and that ageing players were in need of replacement. That is still true, it's just that most of the ageing players have either left or retired.

But United should not be complacent. Juan Mata's goalscoring form appears to have deserted him, and he has missed important and clear chances against both Southampton and Spurs, and is once again fading into anonymity when not given space or runners ahead of him, like a Spanish Shinji Kagawa. Radamel Falcao allegedly didn't stay to watch the match after finding out Van Gaal wanted seventeen defenders on the bench instead of him, because in a Moyes-esque admission, knew he'd have to make defensive changes. Robin Van Persie trundled off, apparently injured, but with him it's hard to tell these days. Antonio Valencia showcased his refound[2] ability to beat players with pace, and showcased his more recent ability of being unable to cross accurately.

There was, however, room for Marouane Fellaini to amble on for the last 20 minutes, which at the time was a reasonable enough choice, but demonstrated just what a waste the first 70 had been. And that's the biggest criticism of Van Gaal's time so far. It isn't the boring football, as unacceptable as that is, because at least he has the excuse that he hasn't had his first choice eleven very often, if at all,

2 And then relost.

and he hasn't had all the players bought that he wanted yet either, and anyway, it's only been six months. No, the biggest criticism is that his substitutions have been largely poor, unable to change the game for anything but the worse.

Which is generally the only thing he's had control over so far, and he's failed. Once he's had a little more time — the fabled two years people claimed to want to give Moyes, for instance — then it's time to judge harshly. For now, his poor substitutions and use of Rooney, a mistake every pundit and manager in the world seems to make, are all we've got to go on. Even a cynic should want to give him enough rope to hang himself with, right now it would barely go round his neck.

There's a potentially bleaker outlook, however. Much the same was being said by level headed onlookers for David Moyes, and eventually it became clear he was in over his head after failing to make the best of a bad job. By March, he was so far buried by his and others' incompetence, that a clean break was needed. That's unlikely to happen with Van Gaal, with a winter transfer window and his own track record hinting we can expect more from United soon enough. There's a shift though, and it's tangible. Now the questions are being asked in the open — how long should he have? How much money will be enough for him? Are his decisions correct? Are his press conferences just bullshit? If we don't know what his philosophy is yet, does he?

Before there was snark, and now there's suspicion, however guarded. The vultures aren't circling, but they did just hear their stomach rumble.

JANUARY 17th

Aston Villa 0-2 Liverpool
Burnley 2-3 Crystal Palace
Leicester 0-1 Stoke
QPR 0-2 Manchester United
Swansea 0-5 Chelsea
Tottenham 2-1 Sunderland
Newcastle 1-2 Southampton

JANUARY 18th

West Ham 3-0 Hull
Manchester City 0-2 Arsenal

JANUARY 19th

Everton 0-0 West Bromwich

There are times when a Diarist's work is unpleasant. Unpleasant but necessary. Others may take the easy road to the obvious conclusion; it is our duty to walk the hard path to the hard truths. If that makes us a pair of modern-day Cassandras, unloved and unheeded in our lifetimes, then so be it. We'll get to be smug after the fact, and that's much more fun.

Arsenal, as you may have heard, beat Manchester City yesterday, a result that was as surprising as the performance was refreshing. Today, then, the newspapers are full of praise for the north London club, for their manager Arsene Wenger, for the team in general, and for a few players in particular.

Not surprising. But totally and utterly wrongheaded. Winning in Manchester was the worst thing that could have happened to Arsenal, and could well destroy their season.

Okay, so they played well. Very well. And in a style of which few thought them capable: they spurned possession, they kept their shape, they made things kind of mucky in midfield, they defended resolutely. Charlton legend Francois Coquelin put himself about in the middle, Olivier Giroud did the same up front, and Laurent Koscielny managed to play 88 minutes plus stoppages on a yellow card, which takes some doing.

And admittedly, they managed to locate a hitherto-undetected, unsuspected ruthlessness, scoring two straightforward goals — a penalty and a header from a free-kick, Arsene? How very Stoke — at two important times in the match. This, along with the rather novel decision to play an adult in goal, reversed the usual Arsenal equation of profligacy at the opposition end, efficient generosity at their own.

And yes, Santi Cazorla was brilliant. Properly, endearingly brilliant, in the way that only a footballer who doesn't look much like an athlete can achieve. We say this not as a criticism — not everybody can attain the sculpted, Adonis-like figure of a highly-toned Diarist — but as the highest of praise; in a game where the bodies are getting increasingly identical, the sight of a chubby-faced, two-footed scamperer dancing his way through midfield is one to make the heart sing, the mouth smile, and the soul do a little jig of celebration.

And fair enough, they made City look fairly ordinary. Well, they helped City make themselves look fairly ordinary. They're an odd team, this City side, exceptionally powerful but very finely-tuned. When everything's humming along in sync they're the most devastating attacking team in the league, even more so than Chelsea, but it doesn't take much in the way of underperformance to knock them off their patterns and force them into relying on moments of individual brilliance. A policy which, unfortunately for Manuel Pellegrini, tends to require either a fully-fit Sergio Aguero or a fully-not-at-the-Africa Cup of Nations Yaya Toure.

And, most importantly, they won! Three points! A move up the table! Ahead of Tottenham, one point behind Manchester United! So close to the promised land of fourth place!

But no. Ignore that; ignore it all. There are times when winning is the right thing to do, and times when it looks hopelessly short-sighted. Arsenal, as everybody knows, have problems. Problems that can only be solved by the immediate purchase of a central defender and a defensive midfielder. Games like this — games that suggest that their current squad is capable of competing with and overcoming the best — are only going to distract from the real matter at hand, which is buying new footballers.

Indeed, what if Wenger decides that this current group of players have demonstrated their ability and earned the right to keep their places? If he decides to buy nobody else at all. Imagine the misery.

Ultimately, this game was literally the only time in modern history where Arsenal would have been better off with Harry Redknapp in charge. For when it comes to playing a bunch of kids in the transfer window, and bouncing his own club into splashing out on the necessary, he's the best in the business.

Oh, Arsene! Look what you've done, you big silly! Football isn't about playing well! It's about shopping! What if you've damaged the shopping?[1]

1 Inevitably, Arsenal fans took this as a face-value attack on their club, leading to an hour weeping at a wall at the sheer pointlessness of it all.

JANUARY 23rd

Cambridge United 0-0 Manchester United

JANUARY 24th

Blackburn Rovers 3-1 Swansea City
Birmingham City 1-2 West Bromwich Albion
Cardiff City 1-2 Reading
Chelsea 2-4 Bradford City
Derby County 2-0 Chesterfield
Manchester City 0-2 Middlesbrough
Preston North End 1-1 Sheffield United
Southampton 2-3 Crystal Palace
Sunderland 0-0 Fulham
Tottenham Hotspur 1-2 Leicester City
Liverpool 0-0 Bolton Wanderers

JANUARY 25th

Bristol City 0-1 West Ham United
Aston Villa 2-1 Bournemouth
Brighton & Hove Albion 2-3 Arsenal

JANUARY 26th

Rochdale 1-4 Stoke City

Thursday 9am, 22 January 2015.
Manuel Pellegrini addresses his squad:
"Right, I've got my suitcases packed. The three exactly the same suits I wear on a rota. The three exactly the same shirts I wear on a rota. The three pairs of exactly the same socks I wear on a rota. The three pairs of exactly the same socks that I wear in whatever order I want, for a bit of fun. It's all fine. I was ready for the flight.

"I've planned everything we need for the trip. I've got the travel board games for you to all to choose from, I've got some stevia chocolate bars as a treat for the winning team of the spelling competition, and I've got extra copies of Shoot! from the newsagents to make sure you're all entertained on the flight. However...

"One of you thought it would be *amusing* to take my passport. We have three hours until our flight leaves, and none of us can go until you give it back. I'm not letting any of you leave until it's returned to me. So, put your hand up, who was it? It's not just my time you're wasting, and I've got all day. I've got as long as it takes."[1]

Friday 6pm, 23 January 2015.
Louis van Gaal addresses his squad:
"For years I went to the doctor to find out what was wrong. I could

1 City had been to Abu Dhabi in the week, to play a mid-season friendly against Hamburg. But they won that 2-0, so it wasn't all bad.

never understand it. It was always there during games — I thought I had something seriously wrong with me. When I won the Champions League, at a time when I should have been celebrating, I was just too stressed out. When I won the Bundesliga, I couldn't relax through the constant distraction.

"And then, at the World Cup, it wasn't there. I'd spent hundreds of thousands of euros on private medical treatment. My premiums were through the roof. I had been beside myself for years, always stressed and belligerent to journalists because of it. And all of a sudden, I felt better. Who'd have known it was so simple? My ass, it stopped twitching when I had three in central defence. It's a totally unheard-of allergy.[2]

"I hope that answers your question, Wayne."

Saturday 12pm, 24 January 2015,
Jose Mourinho addresses the Bradford squad:

"Sorry chaps, but I'm a busy man. I usually just do a handshake a few minutes later, but you know how it is. We're Chelsea and you're just Bradford. No offence, but it would be a disgrace if we lost, the worst defeat of my career, even if I have picked a reserve side.

"So, well done all, thanks for playing. You did yourselves proud, but obviously it's not easy playing against a side with much better funding and, I'm not sorry to say, a special manager. Still, I'm not thinking of the quadruple, no matter what people in the news say. Feel free to take a tour of the ground while you're still here. Do you want an autograph, Phil?"

Sunday 10am, 25 January 2015.
Arsene Wenger addresses his squad:

"OK boys, I've analysed the opposition. They're happy to play on the counterattack and have a few capable players in attack, but as you'd imagine, their defensive is still a little disorganised.

"Tomas and Mesut, make sure you try plenty of through-balls, as they don't have the anticipation or awareness to mark up players with our movement consistently. Tomas, you'll probably be able to find plenty of room just in front of the defence, and Calum, you've the pace to beat your man on the wing, so you'll have plenty of success.

"Theo, make sure you take your shots early — we play at a pace they won't be used to in The Championship. And I'd just like to

2 Not really sure about this, reading it back. Probably should have said "miracle cure".

say to everyone that I'm sorry that I've only just started to address the opposition our strategy. It's much more effective."

Laurent Koscielny wanders in.

"Ah, Laurent, please be on time next week. Anyway, don't worry about you've missed — just play as usual."

Monday 9am, 26 January 2015.
Brendan Rodgers continues to address his squad:
"... Steven is clearly a wonderful and outstanding technician and it's been an honour to have him serve these past three years and it will take serious investment from the board to replace him with someone else who has such an intelligent grasp of the holding role in midfield, and even then it is no guarantee that with such tactically aware players, with superb technique, like Joe Allen and Jordan Henderson — a wonderful human being, too — and Lucas and Emre Can and all the other wonderful players we have who could so ably adapt to Steven's role because that's the kind of understanding we all have amongst ourselves in pursuing brilliance not just for its own sake but because, as Plato said to me when I was his assistant manager, and I think he learned a little from me too ..."

JAN 31st

Hull 0-3 Newcastle
Crystal Palace 0-1 Everton
Liverpool 2-0 West Ham
Manchester United 3-1 Leicester
Stoke 3-1 QPR
Sunderland 2-0 Burnley
West Bromwich 0-3 Tottenham
Chelsea 1-1 Manchester City

FEBRUARY 1st

Arsenal 5-0 Aston Villa
Southampton 0-1 Swansea

The strangest thing happened in the Premier League this weekend. The top of the most exciting, most volatile, most unpredictable, most explosive league in the world suffered a remarkable, astounding, unforeseen, crazy outbreak of something that looks a bit like ... normality? Weird.

Chelsea and City duked one another to a 1-1 draw that, while suiting Chelsea more in terms of the title race, and suiting Mourinho more in his ongoing mission to crush the spirit out of the Premier League like a large man using an overripe grapefruit as a pointed threat, wasn't a terrible result for City. The Champions went to Stamford Bridge in poor form and left with a point, and no amount of exploding citrus fruit can take that away from them. Or can it?

No.

Elsewhere, the rest of the traditional Big Four/Bigger Five/Whopping Five/Colossal Six did their thing in the appropriate fashion. Arsenal, as is their wont, put the hurt on a dreadful team playing dreadfully, and in doing so rekindled that tiny flame of hope that lives inside all Arsenal fans, a warm glow that insists, in the face of all the evidence, that eviscerating somebody useless might, just might, mean something in games against teams that aren't useless. And maybe they're right this time![1]

Manchester United played well for a bit, scored some goals, then played limply for a bit and conceded one. This is an improvement on

1 They were not right.

the last time they played Leicester, and that is the only interesting thing to say about that game. Liverpool welcomed back Daniel Sturridge and watched him do a goal, which bodes well for the month or so between now and that horrible, inevitable moment when he limps off in the last minute of a Europa League tie[2]. Tottenham proved that the magic of Harry Kane is stronger than the magic of Tony Pulis.

But the biggest sign that normality, too, briefly reared its head on the south coast. Southampton have spent all season handily outplaying teams with ease and assurance, and they did precisely the same thing against Swansea, except they forgot to score a goal. Which left the stage clear for perhaps the Premier League most fascinating pair of footballers, Jon and Jo Shelvey, to do their thing. Jon, the sensible one of the pair, drove home the game's only goal from twenty-odd yards; Jo, the amusing liability, fell over a couple of times.

We don't do predictions and we never will steal jokes from Paul Gascoigne, but if we did, we'd boldly claim this weekend as the one where the natural order of things asserted itself. When the Saints, whose marching in has been so impressive, are done. Stick forks in them, if you're feeling particularly upset and curiously violent about it.[3] It's been fun, Southampton, but you can't fight destiny, and you can't fight the natural order of things. This is the Premier League. This is how things are done. Now, eat your proverbial lasagna and sit in your proverbial sick, please.

***

All that predictability at one end, however, only served to really bring out the flavour of the misery going on down below. You know a weekend is shaping up nicely when both Hull City and Aston Villa have managed to catch the eye of the Sky schedulers. There really should be some kind of law against this: when it's a cold winter, and when the country's struggling with sleet and snow and occasional, really weird hailstorms, what kind of sadist puts on not one but two teams made entirely of rain?

Not even good rain. The human capacity for finding patterns and shapes and diversions in almost anything can even make water falling out of the sky something to enjoy, or at least not actively despise.

2 If anything, we hit this prediction too well.

3 One of two outings for this phrase, and due to the quality of the book it is impossible to separate the two.

Gazing out the window into the wet gloom precipitation can, at times, lead to moments of almost transcendental stillness and personal reflection. Or, at least, impromptu races down the window between two exciting drops. Gazing at Hull, on the other hand, brings only a faint nagging sensation in the back of one's mind, the sense that something important has been lost, somewhere, but nothing can ever bring it back.

And walking about in the rain can, given appropriate footwear, be kind of fun, as long as there's good puddles and decent company and maybe somewhere warm to get back to. But when it comes to Villa, and their ongoing war against the idea of goalscoring, all the football fan gets is a cold sogginess of the soul, wet socks, and perhaps, if things go on for too long, some kind of inconvenient illness involving sneezing and Lemsip.

The Premier League doesn't do relegation on meteorological grounds, and that's probably fair enough. But some days it really seems like the right road to be going down, if only for the good of everybody's health. Stay close to your radiators, people, and wrap up warm. There's drizzle out there, and it will do you no good.

FEBRUARY 7th

Tottenham 2-1 Arsenal
Aston Villa 1-2 Chelsea
Leicester 0-1 Crystal Palace
Manchester City 1-1 Hull
QPR 0-1 Southampton
Swansea 1-1 Sunderland
Everton 0-0 Liverpool

FEBRUARY 8th

Burnley 2-2 West Bromwich
Newcastle 1-1 Stoke
West Ham 1-1 Manchester United

FEBRUARY 10th

Arsenal 2-1 Leicester
Hull 2-0 Aston Villa
Sunderland 0-2 QPR
Liverpool 3-2 Tottenham

FEBRUARY 11th

Chelsea 1-0 Everton
Manchester United 3-1 Burnley
Southampton 0-0 West Ham
Stoke 1-4 Manchester City
Crystal Palace 1-1 Newcastle
West Bromwich 2-0 Swansea

Before going to sleep on Sunday night, Louis van Gaal set up his traditional alarm. A course of two million dominoes running from his bedside, around his house and back again, which after precisely eight hours would drop a few of the last dominoes onto his face and wake him up. His wife had never understood why he insisted on doing it this way, but Van Gaal was too stubborn to countenance doing things any other than his way. It worked, so there was no good reason to change things.

As expected, a few dominoes dropped on Van Gaal's face the next morning, and he congratulated himself on his brilliant system he'd formulated. Other people had their alarm clocks or their phones, but that was a ridiculous method in the face of how he did things. He was going to live by his philosophy regardless of what circumstances or outside evidence suggested what he might try instead.

As he washed in his own specially designed bathroom — a thousand heated, wet towels with soap-patches embedded in them for him to roll around in, then another thousand heated, wet towels to rinse off with — he contemplated what he might like for breakfast. "I think today I will have two eggs. It will be a very balanced breakfast, I believe."

And so, with that decided, he began making his breakfast. He took the eggs from the egg pyramid he carefully assembled every week, a fine balance, but in his opinion there was no other way to store eggs. Then he plopped two of them in the kettle, filled it to the brim with water and popped it on. It took a few minutes to boil, but once again, the eggs were perfectly cooked, the yolk just on the cusp of thickening, but still softly set. The kettle looked like it was on its last legs, filled with bits of shell and albumen, so he tossed it in the bin and brought another one out of the cupboard. He went through about 20 a year but he was convinced this was the only way to make eggs properly. His wife and his children used saucepans, but he had no interest in compromising on what he wanted. He finished his plate of coffee quickly — it tended to cool down quicker than in a cup, and he liked that it sped up his morning schedule.

Then, it was time to dress. He put on his club blazer, the one he'd had specifically made from retailoring several club suit trousers into a jacket. He adjusted the club crest on the front, carefully chipped from an ornamental plate, and took out his shoes from the empty fish tank. A cupboard would have been fine, he supposed, but it just wouldn't have felt right. The fish tank meant he could keep an eye on them all week to make sure they were at the desired angle constantly, and he liked the way the little man in the old diving suit peeped out from behind the left brogue.

After driving to the team coach — in reverse, so he could see more clearly the traffic coming towards him from behind — he started to think through the team he'd be picking. Like his morning routine, everything seemed obvious. In midfield he'd pick Wayne Rooney, even if some people had decided he was the club's best striker. Ander Herrera, Juan Mata and Marouane Fellaini would have to sit on the bench to accommodate that move. Anyway, it allowed Robin van Persie and Radamel Falcao to start up front, and he was prepared to allow James Wilson to sit alongside the three midfielder in reserve. Antonio Valencia, the right winger, would start at right back, and Phil Jones, the Phil Jones, in central defence. Perhaps United could have moved for improvements in the January transfer window, but Van Gaal hadn't forced Ed Woodward into action.

As the match started, West Ham battered Manchester United from the outset, taking advantage of a midfield that could not control the game, a captain who could not control the ball or his team, a defence that could not control their own penalty area, and two strikers who could not offer any outlets for a team under pressure. They went a goal down, and looked dead and buried. Then, with two minutes of the match to go, and two minutes into injury time, Daley Blind, the last domino, volleyed in a late equaliser. Manchester United had an away point and remained in the Champions League spots. It had gone just as Van Gaal had always planned.

FEBRUARY 14th (FA CUP)

West Bromwich Albion 4-0 West Ham United
Blackburn Rovers 4-1 Stoke City
Crystal Palace 1-2 Liverpool

FEBRUARY 15th (FA CUP)

Aston Villa 2-1 Leicester City
Bradford City 2-0 Sunderland
Arsenal 2-0 Middlesbrough

FEBRUARY 16th (FA CUP)

Preston North End 1-3 Manchester United

FEBRUARY 21st (LEAGUE)

Aston Villa 1-2 Stoke
Chelsea 1-1 Burnley
Crystal Palace 1-2 Arsenal
Hull 2-1 QPR
Sunderland 0-0 West Bromwich
Swansea 2-1 Manchester United
Manchester City 5-0 Newcastle

FEBRUARY 22nd (LEAGUE)

Tottenham 2-2 West Ham
Everton 2-2 Leicester
Southampton 0-2 Liverpool

This week recalled the worst shameful episodes and weaknesses of football. It was about time that somebody spoke up, and it was perhaps a little galling that it took some spectacularly egregious incidents for them to be listened to, and for the wider world to concede that yes, there might be a problem. It can no longer be swept under the carpet — we've all seen the video, we all know the fallout.

But even then, people denied and obfuscated. People claimed that they weren't sure that the images were showing exactly what were reported. Yes, we could see who was involved, and in this day and age it's easier than ever to identify the culprits, but maybe the exact circumstances, and the intent, were not as clear-cut as it was initially claimed? Of course it looked terrible, but surely nobody would be acting in such a way in the 21st Century? Have things changed so little, onlookers and pundits wondered. But something, as the saying goes, must be done.

And in the age of social media, the defenders remained provocative and pervasive. They got their voice out and spread their own arguments, some of which were picked up by the papers, some of which were mocked by others on the same social media platforms. In America they have a wider culture war, but in Britain it's more about particular groups being targeted. We have our own problems and they can no longer be ignored. The political and commentating classes have failed to properly intervene, and have often made things even worse.

One prominent football man led the complaints for one display of hatred. He went at it so hard and so aggressively that it spooked a satellite channel into changing its lineup on its football analysis flagship show. Of course those providing coverage have to react to the latest news, but it seems somewhat craven to react so quickly in the face of a little bit of pressure and potential controversy when one of the possible guests wants to take on such a vast, hateful problem.

Others wondered about the other incident, when Chelsea disgraced themselves more generally, and pointed out that this was embedded in the history of the club. This wasn't the first time they'd acted with such naked aggression, or tried to intimidate one figure. This wasn't the first time that people in a position of relative authority had abused their privileges, and yet Chelsea had not acted properly in the past to make it clear that this was totally unacceptable and something that needs to be kicked out of football.

Further still, some considered whether that yes, while Chelsea had a long history of involvement in stuff like this, it was a wider problem and one that affected all of football. There is no point limiting the outrage just to how it affects one club, and it prevents a proper root-and-branch appraisal about how to properly tackle the menace. Other clubs have their own stories to tell and their own actions to take, and there needs to be a concerted, organised and honest co-operation to ensure that no longer will we have to realise just how much people can be affected.

And so finally, Jose Mourinho was the man to combat all these ills. He was going to speak up and out on behalf of everyone else. He was mad as hell, and he wasn't going to take it, while looking very sultry, anymore. It was time for someone to bravely take up the campaign and put himself at the forefront, and damn the consequences. He was going to make himself the target against this institutional, structural and personal abuse of a minority — Chelsea football players. Ashley Barnes was just another in a long line of people being taken on, and he strode into the television studio to make his sustained point, for longer than an hour. He made his point and he was breaking the biggest taboos in English football. For too long referees had acted to intimidate others, and he wasn't going to let other distractions — like Chelsea fans singing racist songs and singling out a black man on the Paris metro — get in the way of what was really important.[1]

1 Another one that wasn't run in the Mirror, which is odd, because it's a standard pull-back-and-reveal gag making a fair enough point. In the end, Mourinho had to acknowledge that at the start of the season, when he had said there was no racism in football, that he was talking bollocks. All we're saying is that Mourinho's more on our level. Three high achievers.

FEBRUARY 28th

West Ham 1-3 Crystal Palace
Burnley 0-1 Swansea
Manchester United 2-0 Sunderland
Newcastle 1-0 Aston Villa
Stoke 1-0 Hull
West Bromwich 1-0 Southampton

MARCH 1st

Liverpool 2-1 Manchester City
Arsenal 2-0 Everton

LEAGUE CUP FINAL

Chelsea 2-0 Spurs

MARCH 3rd

Aston Villa 2-1 West Bromwich
Hull 1-1 Sunderland
Southampton 1-0 Crystal Palace

MARCH 4th

Manchester City 2-0 Leicester
Newcastle 0-1 Manchester United
QPR 1-2 Arsenal
Stoke 2-0 Everton
Tottenham 3-2 Swansea
West Ham 0-1 Chelsea
Liverpool 2-0 Burnley

Going into the weekend, the top of the Premier League stood at a fork in the road. Down one well-trodden path lay the familiar, weary outcomes and a dead title race. Down the other lay something more chaotic, more exciting. A world alive with possibility and hope, a future laced with tantalising uncertainty.

Guess which one we chose!

Southampton, just at the moment everybody started taking them seriously as a runner in the Race for A More Profitable European Future, have lost their way. There is a progressive scale of physical inconvenience when it comes to the form of football teams, and Southampton went into the weekend somewhere between Grade 1: Stutter and Grade 2: Hiccup, having won (and, in fact, scored) just once in their last four games. And that was against QPR, who are rubbish.

Not a good time, then, to run into the greatest manager in world football. Koeman got Pulised, Southampton got West Brommed, and Graziano Pelle's soundalike got ever more ironic. The Premier League's breaths of fresh air have progressed beyond Hiccup to Grade Three: Stumble, with Grades Four: Slump and Five: Collapse looming large. Not many football teams make it to Grade Six: Melted Into the Floor and Out of Existence — somebody usually gets sacked first — but we suspect Koeman has enough goodwill stored up from the first half of the season to really give it a shot.

Liverpool, by contrast, have recovered from their own early Grade Four and are, once again, scoring goals, running around quickly, and scaring the sense out of professional footballers who really should know better. Though both sides began in bright fashion, by the end the home side were as effervescent as City were flat; please distribute cause and effect between those two according to taste.

Most of the post-match fallout has focused on City's shortcomings, and rightly so, as the champions got a bit of a slapping. We're living in something of a golden age for limp title defences: while this season is unlikely to top United's Moyesian adventure last season, City are now just five points clear of Arsenal in third, and hopes are high that they can throw this season away even more convincingly than they did in 2012-13[1].

While it would be unfair to single any one individual out for criticism, we don't care: with every passing game, Vincent Kompany looks less like the sensitive, strong, thoughtful centre-half that we all assumed he was, and more like a man doing an insulting impression of Vincent Kompany. At one point he was knocked off the ball by Raheem Sterling. Imagine being knocked off anything by Raheem Sterling, a man who weighs less than his jersey.

Finally, then, to Wembley. It's hard to blame Jose Mourinho for squatting down and relieving himself all over the notion of a fun game: Nemanja Matic was missing, and the last time Chelsea tried to have any fun with Tottenham they found themselves on the wrong end of something hilarious. But still, let's give it a shot.

Come on, Jose! This wasn't about you! This game was about two things. One, making sure Tottenham won the cup so that somebody else could get the taste of champagne, and we could see whether this mystical substance could have the same effect on this young, largely charming Spurs side that it did on his Chelsea the first time around. Second, giving the English press another milestone on the road to tearing Harry Kane to pieces when he fails to win the golden boot at Euro 2016.

But oh no. Jose likes winning trophies and eating trophies and sleeping with trophies and rubbing trophies all over his smouldering, compelling visage. So Jose must have the trophies. While this wasn't quite the perfect day for Mourinho — Arsene Wenger didn't literally or metaphorically fall on his face — you suspect that Roman Abramovich

1 In the end they did something even more damning. They were occasionally excellent, particularly with some individual performances, and showed it's not that they couldn't win, just that they couldn't be bothered to. Pellegrini will stay on next season, too, so well done everyone.

could make a few more tidy billions from his prize asset, if only it were possible to produce electricity from smug.

Overall, then, the top of English football took the opportunity this week to convulse itself into a familiar, predictable shape. Perhaps there is another universe somewhere, one where the title race and the Southampton story and the Tottenham triumph march on. One where it isn't raining. One where she didn't die and leave him alone, rattling around a house built for two. One where he still loves you; one where you still love him. Another place, where we are all unfolding into a better future, a less predictable future, a future where the things that have to happen aren't happening, and so making space for the things that could.

Instead, here, in this universe, where we write and where you read, Chelsea have won the title, Chelsea have won the League Cup, and the race for third and fourth will be between Arsenal, Liverpool and Manchester United. We've walked this way before.

MARCH 7th (LEAGUE)

QPR 1-2 Tottenham

MARCH 7th (FA CUP)

Bradford City 0-0 Reading

Aston Villa 2-0 West Bromwich Albion

MARCH 8th (FA CUP)

Liverpool 0-0 Blackburn Rovers

MARCH 9th (FA CUP)

Manchester United 1-2 Arsenal

14 March 2015 - Birmingham

Reports of unrest in the Midlands started to emerge around the middle of the week, when the national news featured a two minute story on an unusual spike in the number of muggings. Other petty crimes, like vandalism and assault, were also up, and West Midlands Police increased its presence on the street. Nothing much was thought of it at the time, and bigger economic stories and the run-up to the election were drawing more attention.

In the Premier League, Aston Villa visited Sunderland as they attempted to keep the last two matches of resurgence going, to try to build momentum in preparation for their FA Cup semi-final, and to ensure they don't lose focus in the Premier League. Fabian Delph missed the match with a virus, with rumours he could be out for the rest of the season as club doctors could not work out what was exactly wrong with him.

Despite Villa beating Sunderland 1-0, there were rumours of ill-discipline from the Villa team. Alan Hutton and Lee Cattermole spent the whole game kicking lumps out of one another, and it was alleged that Hutton bit the Sunderland midfielder in the tunnel after the game. It was expected that Hutton would face an extensive ban after the referee noted it in his report to the FA.

21 March 2015 - East London

The match between West Ham and Sunderland went ahead despite the stirrings of civil disobedience across the north of England. David

Cameron put the problems down to groups of young men and women who were indulging in 'pure criminality'. Luckily for Sunderland, most of their players did not live in the city centre, and remained unaffected by the disturbances.

There was, though, a serious disturbance to their preparations. Alan Hutton had not only been suspended for biting Lee Cattermole, as expected, but there were rumours of a bust-up with his manager and teammates after the club elected not to appeal the suspension. The club had told him that as he now appeared to be suffering from glandular fever, there would be little point in wasting their time with an appeal, at which time — it is said — he had to be restrained by his teammates as he erupted into an outburst of rage, even foaming at the mouth.

Sunderland demolished West Ham. They played with an intensity and aggression not seen in English football for many years. They were a snarling, barking maelstrom and it appeared that Gus Poyet had finally found some way of getting his side to play for one another. There was even at one point a 30-man brawl as the two sides and the touchline got involved, and at one point Costel Pantilimon even struck a supporter who got too close for comfort, giving him a bloody nose.

On the coach back to Sunderland, the players were warned that Sunderland was under martial law, with fires breaking out in the city centre.

4 April 2015 - Birmingham

West Ham's players had to make their way to the game by helicopter as the main roads across Britain were, as they had been for the last few days, suffering from a traffic crisis. They didn't realise at the time, but they would be taking part in one of the last games of football in Britain for the foreseeable future.

In response to the utter chaos in the Midlands, which one journalist insisted had been building ever since Fabian Delph was bitten by the wild crowds of Villa fans celebrating an FA Cup quarter-final victory, the government decided that football matches could only go ahead behind closed doors. Riot police were called to hold the thronging masses of supporters at bay outside Leicester's ground, but the police were confident that they could keep a couple of hundred irate fans at bay.

They were wrong. Just as the second half began, the mob broke through the police lines. Hundreds and hundreds of disgruntled Leicester citizens burst through into the match, tearing through the ground and smashing up doors, offices, searching for anyone they could find.

It was the same across the country, and not just in football grounds. Cities were on fire. The police had lost control of the situation and the army was called up, despite reports that in some regiments, squaddies had turned on their officers. The first stories began to come through of people being eaten, actually eaten, in the street. The British population had turned feral. The stories stopped when the BBC signal went off air, and by the end of the day radio was nothing more than white noise with the occasional panicked interruption from state emergency services, broadcasting on any channel they could find.

13 November 2017, UN report summary

We now know that the man who bit Fabian Delph was Patient Zero. We do not know how or why — we suspect he had been spat on a few days before — but he had become infected with a virus that turned anyone who comes in contact with it into a rampaging zombie-like figure. From there, thanks to their cross-country travel and tendency to collect in crowds, football clubs and their fans transmitted the virus in a matter of weeks, before it was too late. We do not know when the infection will stop, or if the UK will ever become habitable again.

Ultimately, and considering the difficulty in securing the entire North European coastline, we must reluctantly agree with our colleagues in the US Air Force. Operation Cleansing Hellfire is the only available solution.[12]

1 This was also not run by The Mirror. We're not sure if pretending Fabian Delph was at the heart of a zombie outbreak is libellous or not, but we're not the experts.

2 While there was something very Nu Football about the resurgence of pitch invasions, the outcry that met them was predictably ridiculous, someone-could-have-been-killed Helen Lovejoy complaining. Still, at least it makes a change from the worst of Nu Football — hoping that young people die so they can be conspicuously mourned in public.

MARCH 14th

Crystal Palace 3-1 QPR

Arsenal 3-0 West Ham

Leicester 0-0 Hull

Sunderland 0-4 Aston Villa

West Bromwich 1-0 Stoke

Burnley 1-0 Manchester City

MARCH 15th

Chelsea 1-1 Southampton

Everton 3-0 Newcastle

Manchester United 3-0 Tottenham

MARCH 16th

Swansea 0-1 Liverpool

You won't be reading this anywhere else this Monday, but Manuel Pellegrini is a genius. The Chilean replaced chippy scarf-model Roberto Mancini in the hope that he could bring a more "holistic" management style to Manchester City. On Saturday we learned just how far he is willing to take this mission.

City lost to Burnley. This might be considered something of a shock, seeing as one side carries a price tag that wouldn't shame an aircraft carrier while the other was assembled in exchange for a couple of badly-painted Airfix, but Pellegrini's never cared for the odds. George Boyd scored a really rather cute winner, and while City should probably have had a penalty later in the game, the way things were going Sergio Aguero would almost certainly have passed it square.

In itself, and in terms of their ailing title defence, an appalling result. City are now six points behind Chelsea — who have a game in hand — and, more amusingly just one point ahead of Arsenal and two ahead of Manchester United. But that's not the holistic picture.

In essence, it became clear that City weren't going to be winning the league again this season after they caught Chelsea, then allowed them to get away. Fine. Now, a less holistic manager than Pellegrini might have happily accepted the comfortable second place that he was being handed; keep things ticking over, coast home, make lots of apologetic shrugging gestures in the direction of Chelsea, and maybe keep his job. But not our Manuel! Oh no.

See, Pellegrini knows what holisticity means. Holisticism, despite the strange disappearance of the 'w', is about the whole picture, about the interconnectedness of all things[1], and the whole picture looks far more entertaining this morning. His loss — his team's loss — is everybody else's gain: the fans of United and Arsenal, the neutrals who just want to see interesting things happen, and the sponsors and television companies and everybody else who has a stake in the ongoing fiction that the Premier League is the Best in the World. It isn't. But it can sometimes be exciting.

He's not doing it on purpose, of course. That would be an allegation of throwing football matches, and that sort of thing gets lawyers very excited and Diarists very spiked. No, this isn't deliberate; it's more fundamental than that. The powers that be at City might well have thought that holisticality might just be a cheap, fancy-sounding word slogan, a handy euphemism for suits who can't quite bring themselves to admit 'we sacked the last bloke because he was, frankly, an [redacted]'.

They should have paid more attention. They accidentally ended up with somebody who was so damn holistical that he couldn't help but take the needs of the wider country to heart. We can't have a race for first, he realised. Let's have one for second, third and fourth. Hell, if Southampton's squad can hold out, if Tottenham can avoid turning into Spurs, and if Liverpool don't vanish up Brendan's inverted commas again, then let's get fifth, sixth and seventh involved as well.

They wanted a man who didn't irritate the majority of his squad, didn't wear a scarf like it was some kind of weapon, and didn't wear a scarf like some kind of weapon. They wanted a man who would work amiably with those above and below him, who would keep things ticking over pleasantly off the field and pleasingly on. Instead, they got a man who can do most of that, sometimes, but is fundamentally a servant to the mysterious forces of holisticience. Here to make the world a better place, for everybody. It might cost him his job. But it's perked the Premier League up no end, and for that, Manuel, we salute you.

***

Down at the other end, Tim Sherwood's been having fun at Gus Poyet's expense. While we at the Diary have little love for the hapless Uruguayan — never trust a man with a personalised snood, as a wise

1 Which is different from David Cameron's Internet of Things. Though he does put the the hole into holistic.

fortune cookie once said — the spectacle of Sherwood clearing the dust from Villa's corridors is strangely compelling. Look at those footballers, previously the most miserable in the land, running around and smiling. Who knew that management could, in essence, amount to charging into a football club, clapping a lot, and insisting everybody start having fun immediately?

Okay, so it's probably a bit more complicated than that. But not by much.

Still, everything moves in cycles, and a forcible insistence on everybody having fun only lasts as long as everybody can remember the miserable bloke who came before. So here's what we suggest. Tim Sherwood and Paul Lambert both sign five-year contracts to manage Aston Villa, but do so on the understanding that they take it in turns, on rotation, switching jobs just after Christmas when the other bloke's powers wear off. From giddy chirpmeister to dour tactician and back again, never allowing the other time to get stale, always keeping things fresh. If you're interested, Randy, and would like further details, do feel free to get in touch. Our rates are reasonable. Invoice via Mirror Towers.

MARCH 21st

Manchester City 3-0 West Bromwich
Aston Villa 0-1 Swansea
Newcastle 1-2 Arsenal
Southampton 2-0 Burnley
Stoke 1-2 Crystal Palace
Tottenham 4-3 Leicester
West Ham 1-0 Sunderland

MARCH 22nd

Liverpool 1-2 Manchester United
Hull 2-3 Chelsea
QPR 1-2 Everton

Half time: Welcome back to live minute-by-minute coverage of the match between Liverpool and Manchester United. United went into an early lead through a well worked goal from Juan Mata, who converted smartly from Ander Herrera's excellent through ball. United dominated the early stages of the match, but Liverpool started to edge things as they grew into the half — and they went very close to an equaliser when Adam Lallana fired just wide of the near post.

The second half is imminent
We're getting news that Adam Lallana, who was thunderously clattered by Phil Jones when the two of them challenged for a high ball, has had to go off injured, to be replaced by Steven Gerrard.

The whole of the ground will be looking to Gerrard to inspire his side in what is almost certainly his very last game against Manchester United at Anfield. The stage is set for a dramatic send off for him, perhaps another memory to add to the FA Cup final and Istanbul?

45:01 - Yep, here's Gerrard now, coming onto the pitch. He's got the captain's armband. The one he's famous for, the one he's earned, the one he deserves for the years of service to Liverpool. The crowd are roaring. Can he give them one more parting gift?

45:02 - The ball is is worked back to Gerrard from the centre circle, and it looks like he'll be playing the midfield anchor role.

It's a role that he's adapted to as his body has started to fade with age. A lot like Andrea Pirlo and Paul Scholes, as he's lost the stamina of youth, Brendan Rodgers has exploited his experience to move him back into the midfield pivot position, a quarterback if you will. From here he should be able to start attacking moves.

45:15 - Gerrard is haring around, in fact, swapping passes in midfield. No sign of any faded energy here! He's launching yet another of his trademark crossfield balls to get things going.

45:21 - The ball is brilliantly brought down on the right wing and returned to Gerrard in the centre of the park. He's got Liverpool moving with a renewed purpose here. The whole team are raising their game to match his high standards. The game is absolutely set up for him to dominate, and he's doing it.

45:25 - What a challenge! Oof! Classic Gerrard! Receiving a loose pass in midfield, Mata starts to close him down. There's a chance of a counterattack here if the Spaniard can get to it first, but Gerrard slides firmly straight through him, and wins the ball at the same time. It was a little bit of a risk to go in so hard, with referees as harsh as they are these days, but he used his encyclopaedic knowledge of the game to understand there's a little leeway in the febrile atmosphere of the Liverpool-United game.

45:27 - This just in from our reporter at the ground. Can Liverpool really afford to lose his experience? His knowhow? This decision could haunt the club for a few seasons yet, especially should he come back on loan to other clubs from LA. It's hard to imagine this place without him. The crowd absolutely loved that challenge, they're really fired up. Anfield is rocking.

45:30 - Gerrard still at the centre of things, thirty seconds into the half. Absolutely everything is going through the captain so far. He lays one pass forward and Herrera slides into him aggressively to close down his pass, which he manages to get away. Herrera was obviously giving a little back after Mata was on the receiving end. Tough but fair stuff.

45:32 - Dirty foreigners

The referee's whistled here, and Herrera is down in pain. Presumably he's in trouble for that reckless lunge towards Gerrard — you don't necessarily have to make contact to give away a foul. Herrera's trying the old trick of feigning injury in an attempt to avoid punishment.

45:38 - RED CARD! STEVEN GERRARD HAS BEEN SENT OFF! Gerrard has been sent off for stamping on Herrera as he slid past him. It was as plain as day, and that's it for the captain

45:41 - Oh no, look at this.[1]

45:50 - The armband's off now.

1 This is a reference to Martin Tyler watching Steven Gerrard be sent off, to which his reaction was an embarrassing, "Oh no," having found it impossible not to betray his unhappiness. That's not to say Tyler is a fervent ABU or a Liverpool fan, but he — along with everyone in prominent media positions and no other neutrals — had decided that this season would end in a fairytale for dear Steven. Quite why they wanted it, when Gerrard is the height of footballing solipsism, is an interesting question — the answer probably being that pundits don't understand the average fan just likes making fun of footballers, not praising them. And when Gerrard fucked up yet again, trying to bend the modern football game to his anachronistic approach, everyone got the chance to mock him one more time. Still, at least he didn't slip again.

MARCH 27th

England 4-0 Lithuania

MARCH 31st

Italy 1-1 England

Before we get underway with the diary today, let's make one thing clear — one of us is ill. Not dreadfully ill[1] — there is no need to worry (or if you don't like us, hope) — it is simply a virus that causes snot, phlegm, nosebleeds and fever. Oh, the fever! The looping dreams have become absurd and disorientating, with one of us located in a demi-monde of unspeakable languages that all, for reasons inexplicable, focus on peer-to-peer lending interest rates and what that might mean for the future. It is with that in mind that we ask you to understand the prism of wretchedness through which we watched Harry Kane and England defeat Lithuania.

Lithuania, whose biggest claim to fame is that it makes you go, "Dodgy taxation practices? Ah, no, that's Lichtenstein. Lithuania, Baltics, got it."

Now, through the fever and illness it's quite difficult to remember just what happened. But we know that Kane shone through with a brilliance that was unparalleled, scoring in just slightly more seconds than it took for Steven Gerrard to be sent off in the previous weekend. Though the game might have already been settled, with goals from Wayne Rooney, Danny Welbeck and Raheem Sterling.

Rooney's goal, heading in a rebound, meant that he is now just two away from equalling the record of Bobby Charlton's 49 international

1 It turned out one of us was actually really unwell, for a month, with a chest infection, and this wasn't helped by drinking for six hours with the other one; the joy of booze kidding him that actually, he was fine. Just say no, kids.

goals[2]. He also managed to hit the woodwork twice, as some kind of metaphor of him setting up basecamp halfway to success, only to decide he'd rather just take a few photos of the mountain's peak rather than climbing any further. If there is a man who will look back on statistics in favour of remembering how he wasted his thrilling talent, it will be Rooney. Captain? Yep. Leader? Erm. Legend? Let's look at a dictionary to see the definition of that before we make any decisions.

England have, undeniably, hit form in their European Championship qualifying group. They've played five and won five. They've conceded just two goals in their last seven matches, since coming back from predictable disappointment at the World Cup. Danny Welbeck has six goals for England in the qualification stage, despite being a relative rank incompetent for Manchester United first, Arsenal second. England are definitely going to qualify for the European Championships, and it is only the players and manager who have any differing opinion to us on how we all know it will really play out.

England will win almost every single one of their qualifying group games. They will be congratulated for their professional performances away to sides in Eastern Europe, but they will be reminded that the "hard work starts in earnest now". ("Now" being the end of qualification. Not actually now. This explanation is harder work than England's qualifying group.) "Now", as they draw in two unsatisfactory friendlies against Chile and Estonia, before finishing off with an inspiring victory over a second string Spain side, Real Madrid's David de Gea throwing one in. They will be drawn in the group stage against Italy, Greece and Poland.

They will beat Greece 2-1 in their opening match after falling behind to a Chris Smalling own goal, before Rooney equalises and the substitute Kane scores a scuffed winner. There will be clamour for Kane to start against Poland, and he will. He will miss two easy shots as the pressure gets to him, before crossing for Danny Welbeck, dropped to accommodate him, to equalise.

That will leave England up against Italy to squeeze through, in a battle to get more than four points to progress. England will lose 2-0 and Phil Jones will be sent off for a slightly dodgy but ultimately deserved second yellow, which allows Andrea Pirlo to repeat his spot-kick humiliation of Joe Hart. The loudest English voices will cry foul, and Roy Hodgson will go on for another full year in charge

2 One now. In a touching tribute to the man whose record he's about to break, he's going bald for the seventh time.

of England, before resigning over the tear-stained pages of an award-winning paperback. Harry Kane's scoring chart will eventually progress to match a reverse Fibonacci sequence[3].

This is all obvious, it is all clear and pre-destined. It is the same thing as the sickness, confused statistics that on the surface appear to make sense, until you dive down the rabbit hole of trying to define what exactly should be going on. And that's when you realise what supporting England is: a looping fever dream, a demi-monde of unspeakable languages that all, for reasons inexplicable, focus on peer-to-peer lending interest rates and what that might mean for the future. However many goals Kane and Rooney might score for England.

3 Exactly what the reverse of an infinite sequence of numbers looks like is something that only makes sense while in the claws of illness. Just go with it.

APRIL 4th

Arsenal 4-1 Liverpool
Everton 1-0 Southampton
Leicester 2-1 West Ham
Manchester United 3-1 Aston Villa
Swansea 3-1 Hull
West Bromwich 1-4 QPR
Chelsea 2-1 Stoke

APRIL 5th

Burnley 0-0 Tottenham
Sunderland 1-0 Newcastle

APRIL 6th

Crystal Palace 2-1 Manchester City

APR 7th

Aston Villa 3-3 QPR

Eighteen minutes. Well, thirty-three if you include half-time. Probably more like thirty-five, thinking about it, since there's first half injury time to consider. That's how long it took for Loic Remy and Chelsea to regain the lead after Charlie Adam's misplaced pass was carried into Thibaut Courtois' net by a passing pigeon. That's how long the title race was alive, and that's not bad, since it's been dead for months. Even Jesus only managed 40 days, and he'd been dead barely a weekend.

That was your obligatory Easter joke. We hope you enjoyed it.

While it might seem, on the surface, that Chelsea were ruining everybody else's fun, it's worth considering the alternative. A resurrected title race would mean taking Arsenal seriously as contenders, and it's far too late in the season for an effort of that magnitude.

The Gunners recent good form has been almost David Frost-like in its frictionlessness; they've risen without trace as those around them have been messing about elsewhere, and all of a sudden they're the best in the country and nobody really knows why or how. Your typical metropolitan elite, basically. Somebody — nobody seems quite sure if it was Alan Bennett or Peter Cook, and nobody seems quite sure if it was a joke — once said that their greatest regret was saving David Frost from drowning. We can be thankful that Remy is not cursed with such a soft heart.

***

Liverpool also managed about half an hour, before collapsing gently and sadly into themselves like an origami crane left out in bad weather. According to this very newspaper, their capitulation at Arsenal was followed by a full and frank sharing of views behind the scenes, which we can only assume went something like this:

RODGERS: You fools! That's the race for fourth completely shafted! What on earth are you playing at?
PLAYERS: Oh dear. We hadn't thought of that. We've let the whole league down here.
RODGERS: Simon, can you play wingback?[1]

***

Fortunately for us all, just as the title race dies (again) and the Race For The Chance To Get Done By Barcelona starts to look very unwell indeed, the relegation stramash leaps jauntily back to life. And quite right too: this has not been a season worthy of an exciting finish at the good end of the table, because there hasn't really been a good end of the table. This is a season which deserves to end with Hull and Aston Villa slogging it out in front of a tired, uncaring nation, desperately flailing at one another in the hope that they might just be slightly less useless than the other lot.

With due deference to Leicester's excellent win over the lingering smell that is West Ham and Jermain Defoe's tap-in against Newcastle, with a wave towards Burnley's soul-sapping grind against Spurs, and with nods of acknowledgement towards Villa and Hull's losses, this weekend takes the Diary into un-Diarised waters. Where no Diary has gone before. Where Diaries fear to tread.

We need to talk about Queens Park Rangers.

It wasn't a glamorous game, like a World Cup semi-final or a Champions League second leg, and so it's not going to get the love when these lists get made, but we still need to consider the question: was this the most surprising football result of all time? Let's consider the facts:

QPR are basically rubbish: they haven't scored four goals all season and they've only scored three once, against — oh, look! — West Brom, back in December. But that was West Brom under Alan Irvine, and they weren't very good ...

1 For any of you out there that can draw, we've checked and nobody's yet taken brendanrodgersaskingthingsiftheycanplaywingback.tumblr.com.

... whereas West Brom under Tony Pulis have been much better, because Tony Pulis is the best manager in the world. More to the point, he's the best manager in the world[2] because he can, given just two toilet roll tubes, some pipecleaners and a lot of sticky back plastic, produce a defence of admirable sturdiness and grit. The kind of defence that absolutely does not concede four to Queens Park Rangers ...

... particularly not Queens Park Rangers away from home, where they have been the square root of miserable all season. Their only other points on the road came in February against the rotting corpse of Gus Poyet; this, by contrast, was a tricky journey to a decent team ...

... which they overcame, in part, thanks to a goal from Bobby Zamora that would have shamed Michael Laudrup with its insolent, impudent charm. That's Bobby Zamora. That's Michael Laudrup. It's an overused word, but that's bordering on the miraculous.

We know where all the evidence is pointing. We know what time of year it is. We know what you're thinking. Is Chris Ramsey the second coming of Jesus? Well, you can't spell Christ without Chris ... but it's not for us to say.

2 Not even joking. He's great. And he would absolutely piss the Bundesliga.

APRIL 11th

Swansea 1-1 Everton

Southampton 2-0 Hull

Sunderland 1-4 Crystal Palace

Tottenham 0-1 Aston Villa

West Bromwich 2-3 Leicester

West Ham 1-1 Stoke

Burnley 0-1 Arsenal

APRIL 12th

QPR 0-1 Chelsea

Manchester United 4-2 Manchester City

APRIL 13th

Liverpool 2-0 Newcastle

Big day on Sunday. Two local rivals met in the kind of game that sees the nation's thesauruses stretched to breaking point. It was titanic (except nobody died). It was cataclysmic (except nobody was buried in a catacomb, at a guess[1,2,3]). It was slightly lacking in fundamental quality (because this is the Premier League). It was, ultimately, of no relevance to the destination of the title. But it was useful for anybody having to write about the weekend, because everybody loves one of those hilarious, in-no-way telegraphed false introductions. Yes, Chelsea went to QPR.

Wait! Come back! We're sorry; we couldn't help ourselves; we'll get to the good stuff in a bit. For now, we should note that while we still don't have a title race, the windows for pretending that we do are getting larger. Last week, It Was On for about half an hour, until Chelsea took the lead. This week, we got nearly twenty hours of proper rollercoaster: from the end of Arsenal's comprehensive 1-0 thrashing of Burnley, through the thrilling moment that Loic Remy felt tightness in his calf, and on into the pulsating exchanges of the West London Derby.

Okay, so QPR's cauldron of hate felt more like a soupbowl of peevishness. And yes, those exchanges were pulsating in an nauseating,

---

1 As any fule kno, catacomb has Latin roots, whereas cataclysm is from the Greek for deluge, kataklusmos, but we can't resist the banter (late 17th century, origin unknown).

2 Your mum's late 17th century, origin unknown.

3 That really didn't work.

poisonous way, like a boil, or rice pudding. And of course, Cesc Fabregas turned up at the end to ruin the whole thing. But still! Twenty hours of hot title action! At this stage of the season! No wonder Manchester City's players looked knackered.

***

Speaking of false openings, the Manchester derby finally put to bed all the suggestions that City have mysteriously forgotten how to play well. For ten minutes they rolled back the years — er, year — and made United's defence look like two midfielders, a buffoon, and Chris Smalling. In went their goal. Up went their spirits. 'Oh,' went Old Trafford. 'Oh dear.'

Then they stopped.

We can only assume that the sight of Ashley Young bettering Dennis Bergkamp's greatest and most accidental goal would, at close quarters, have been profoundly disturbing. But the immediacy with which they went from CITY! to City? made it look almost like a downing of tools. Like they'd made their point — we can play football, see? — and then decided that, with their point made, they didn't need to keep going on about it. Like a macro version of Dimitar Berbatov: I think I can, I know I can, I sometimes do, so piss off.

Even Vincent Kompany's brush with a red card was born less from the appropriate overflow of derby violence, and more from a pain in his leg and ego. We're not saying City have entirely chucked the season in, but we are heavily and obviously implying that.

***

Of course, there could only be one choice for Man of the Match. Ashley Young was excellent, Juan Mata was adorable, and Marouane Fellaini was excellent in his new, highly specialised role as a steam-powered robot teetering on the edge of explosion. But there is only one Michael Carrick, and that's just as well.

When Carrick plays well, half the people are pleased; these are the people who hold him up as the Geordie Xavi, a deep-playing playmaking genius who has only been kept from the Ballon d'Or by the barbaric footballing culture in which he is forced to wallow. And when he plays badly, the other half are pleased; these are the people that view him as one of football's great modern frauds, a defensive liability whose positive attributes are consistently overstated by idiots desperate to pretend that this miserable, rain-sodden island can produce a Xavi of its very own.

Carrick did his very best to prove both sides correct. There he was for City's opening goal, standing around uselessly while the gorm drained from his body and David Silva skipped away. And there he was once United woke up, pinging the ball around nicely. Whatever else Carrick might be, he seems a pleasant man, and here he was giving everybody something to get their teeth into. In your face, Abraham Lincoln. You can fool all the people all the time.

***

Finally, a note for United victorious manager, who may have won the tactical battle but has made a serious strategic error. For perhaps the first time in twenty-odd years, Manchester United's fanbase went into a season making all manner of strange noises. Noises about just wanting to get back in the top four. Noises about not really anticipating a title challenge. Modest noises. Sensible noises.

So as United approached their recent run of tricky fixtures, Van Gaal had an opportunity. A bit of a fumble here, a bit of a slip there ... with careful management and a bit of luck, United could achieve their back-into-Europe goal while still retaining the air of an imperfect, sputtering machine. Expectations could be kept nice and low; works could be held very much in progress. Pressure could be averted.

Instead, the silly fool has gone and beaten Liverpool away and City at home in entertaining, convincing fashion. Now Old Trafford is bouncing and the giddiness is back. Sure, the points might look good now. But he's only made the job harder for himself in the long term. Take a tip for the Diary, Louis. First, set yourself the lowest possible targets. Then, and only then, can you get away with consistently failing to achieve them.[4]

4 That you are reading this means that we achieved our only target with the last book: not losing so much money that Hartrick's publishing company had to shut down.

APRIL 18th (LEAGUE)

Crystal Palace 0-2 West Bromwich

Everton 1-0 Burnley

Leicester 2-0 Swansea

Stoke 2-1 Southampton

Chelsea 1-0 Manchester United

APRIL 19th (LEAGUE)

Manchester City 2-0 West Ham

Newcastle 1-3 Tottenham

FA CUP SEMI-FINALS [BOTH IN LONDON]

APRIL 18th

Reading 1-2 Arsenal [aet]

APRIL 19th

Aston Villa 2-1 Liverpool

The world of football is blessed with players who, in their careers and during retirement, went by just a single name. Like Prince, a single-phrase moniker was all that was needed to tell people who they were, and who commentators were referring too. They were mainly Brazilian, with players like Pele, Socrates, Tostao, Romario, Ronaldo and Ronaldinho all excellent examples. There was also Eusebio, of course, who lit up the 1966 World Cup as much as any English player did during the tournament. What the single-name name means is that the player transcends normal means of recognition, and that they are so pre-eminent that they are not just footballers, they are celebrities. World figures off the back of their talents and achievements.

What should not be escaped though is the quiet revolution in the north west of England, where something similar has taken place over the last couple of years. Talent and achievement are words that do not do justice to the two footballing celebrities. No, they stretch across the world under their own shortened names: Brendan and Steven. And once again, as Liverpool went to the famous Wembley Stadium, Brendan and Steven demonstrated just what it is about them that makes them so instantly recognisable and respected by everyone involved in football and, indeed, beyond.

The game against Aston Villa was a massive game for Steven, we were all told every day for the last three months, because Steven was having his birthday on the day of the FA Cup final, and we were again told every three months that the neutrals across Britain so wanted to see Steven play his final match for Liverpool and to pick up a trophy at the same time. This followed last season, when the neutral was told that given Steven was now in his thirties, it would be so wonderfully fitting for him to lift the Premier League trophy as he was destined to do. It was in the stars, and as the pundits on Match of the Day, and the opinion formers in the national papers decided, it was the right thing to happen. Rarely was it mentioned that Steven might not actually be good enough, and had done nothing to actually deserve any trophy that he hadn't already won.

Which is what made Steven's collapse against Chelsea last season so incredibly funny. After being told so long what people should want to happen, it turns out most people just wanted to point at laugh as someone who was so demonstrably keen on themselves. This is England, after all, where a national pastime is to point and laugh at anyone who might consider themselves marginally above average, regardless of that being the truth or otherwise[1].

And so it happened again at the weekend. Steven was unable to battle his way past a tactically sophisticated Aston Villa, despite being the very best holding midfielder in Europe, and a casual glance at the neutrals' actual opinions, rather than the neutrals' opinions as filtered through what they are supposed to be, revealed that yep, actually, it is still very funny to see him, forehead creased in confusion at his own failure, like a bird that's just flown into a window.

His partner in crime, Brendan, must take some of the blame for his own cowardice. Instead of managing Steven as he should — by replacing him last season — he has taken the soft option, and chivvied him along occasionally, all while being criticised by both those who take look at Steven and see a Pele, and those who look at Steven and see nothing of any use at all. Despite Steven's disruptive approach to contract negotiations, done during a paper interview when it became clear he wasn't going to get what he wanted, he decided that it wasn't worth the hassle of making it clear Steven no longer deserved a place in the Liverpool squad, and certainly not in the first team.

Instead, Brendan allowed the situation to fester, and praised him to the hilt while conspicuously readying himself for his departure by giving no contract extension. He continued to play him in important games, and was rewarded by a red card against Manchester United, and then a wretched display against Aston Villa. The Brendan

1 cf. Lewis Hamilton: incredibly talented, but all anyone does in England is mock his silly outfits (rightly).

and Steven show, an exercise in style over substance, has been the downfall of Liverpool this season, and now Steven has nothing to show for it. Again.

It doesn't mean he wasn't an excellent player. It doesn't mean from his fans' point of view, and his own, that it isn't sad that for all the effort he's made for Liverpool that he wasn't able to win a Premier League with them, or one last cup. But what it really means, above all else, is that when it comes down to it, all the neutral football fan wants is to point and laugh at someone, anyone, thank you very much.

APRIL 25th

Southampton 2-2 Tottenham

Burnley 0-1 Leicester

Crystal Palace 0-2 Hull

Newcastle 2-3 Swansea

QPR 0-0 West Ham

Stoke 1-1 Sunderland

West Bromwich 0-0 Liverpool

Manchester City 3-2 Aston Villa

APRIL 26th

Everton 3-0 Manchester United

Arsenal 0-0 Chelsea

APRIL 28th

Hull 1-0 Liverpool

APRIL 29th

Leicester 1-3 Chelsea

It will all be over soon. The question of whether this season of Premier League: Football Bonanza! is the worst season of Premier League: Football Bonanza! is one that we must leave for the historians. We are too close to the action to call it, though it's the end of April and as things stands, there is exactly one interesting thing happening.

***

It's not at the top, though it's a question of taste whether Chelsea themselves are boring (the Diary's view on this particular Monday morning is that any deficit in on-pitch style is more than made up in the off-field whingefest that they seem to provoke). Let's not forget that it's games that are boring, not teams — you'll recall that Chelsea were exceptionally entertaining against Paris Saint-Germain not too long ago — and it takes two to Tizer. Let's also not forget that the only thing more boring than being boring is going on about being boring. And let's, therefore, say no more about it.

Let's not waste any time talking about the game, either, which stands as a neatly emblematic 90 minutes for the entire season. Last time was about Liverpool's crazy dash for the title; the one before was an Alex Ferguson appreciation procession. But this time, it's all about two things: Chelsea having already done enough to win, and penalties. Even with Arsenal in their best form in living memory of children, and even with some hot jazz refereeing, the result here was precisely as anticipated, and precisely in the manner anticipated. Only

Chelsea's celebrations showed any hint of life, and we're working on the assumption that they were trying to irritate Thierry Henry.

***

Vague hints of life threatened to re-enter the race for fourth; at least, they did if you watched the weekend in reverse order. (Even better: watch the actual games backwards? Reverse time, and each game begins as a chaotic mess; then tidies itself; then ends with a perfect 0-0 draw; everybody's equal, and alphabetical order means Arsenal finally get their hands on a title.)

So if Everton's 3-0 dissection of a miserable Manchester United had come before Liverpool's dire 0-0 game against West Brom, then the former (though actually the latter) would have been a door opening. Opportunity knocking on that open door. Opportunity realising that you don't need to knock on an open door; you can just go in. Not that this would have made Liverpool's performance more interesting, of course; nothing short of powerful narcotics could have managed that. This would, yes, simply have tricked everybody into thinking that both games were more important than they were. However, that would have been something.

***

Any other manager, and Leicester's run of victories would have served our purpose here. Nigel Pearson, though, while he's certainly doing some fine work, has at all times an off-putting air of obsessional healthiness, of cross country runs in the biting winter air, of a firm and immovable belief that there's only one path to heaven, and that path goes through ditches and over hills and is murder on the knees. Keeping Leicester up would be a fine achievement. Getting them here was too. Only thing is, he scares the hell out of us[1].

***

Desperate times call for desperate measures. For the breaking of all the rules. Our policy here at the Diary has always been that we don't actively want anybody to go down, unless (a) they're managed

1 So much so that we named this book in tribute to him. Please stop staring at us like that, Nigel.

by somebody we don't like (b) it would be funny, or (c) we're just in a bad mood[2]. Right now, though, we need Newcastle to go down, and we need Newcastle to go down not just for their own good, but everybody's else's as well.

Consider: while Mike Ashley's decision to run the club as an investment fund might be appalling on every moral, aesthetic and sporting level, it makes perfect sense. Righteousness is one thing: the realisation that the Premier League can be treated like the London property market quite another. If Ashley successfully demonstrates that increased television deals will come to anybody able to keep a club just above the mire as cheaply and as lifelessly as possible, then we can guarantee he won't be the last.

Consider: a Premier League consisting of three or four teams fighting the drop, four or five scrapping for the European places, and everybody else existing in a strange limbo, devoted to the business of staying a Premier League club purely because staying a Premier League club is good business. Kind of like now, but much, much worse. Even though Newcastle seem okay, as these things go, they absolutely must secure an unlikely relegation[3]. That's the last thing we've got to cling to: this shambles of an owner cannot be permitted to be correct.

*** AVIAN INTERLUDE ***

Football people have a funny relationship with our feathered friends. For every Eric Cantona, able to call upon a flock of seagulls to gently yet insistently embarrass the media, there's a Joe Kinnear, who once told national radio that he wasn't bothered, that he didn't care, that it was all just "water off a duck's arse".

But this doesn't scare Nigel Pearson. Nothing scares Nigel Pearson, as far as we can tell; this is a man who told the Telegraph's Henry Winter that he once, while on holiday, fought off a pack of wild dogs with only a pair of walking poles. The natural world holds no fear for him. And nor does the bearpit of the press conference.

To recap. Pearson was holding forth about Leicester City having received unfair criticism for being rubbish when a journalist named

2 As such, we want everybody to go down, all of the time, except Swansea.

3 You look at John Carver, and you know you can't joke. It feels mean to even pity him. Still, at least Steve McClaren is an expert when it comes to brand management and public relations. Newcastle fans will no doubt love him — perhaps in interviews he'll do his own little Geordie accent.

Ian Baker asked what unfair criticism he meant. Pearson first accused him of having his head in the clouds, before before than screeching wildly across the lanes of the highway of metaphor and informing him that "If you don't know the answer to that question then I think you are an ostrich. Your head must be in the sand. Is your head in the sand? Are you flexible enough to get your head in the sand? My suspicion would be no."

Amusing on the page; actually quite terrifying in real life, apparently, at least when coming from a man who makes kebabs out of dogs while out for a stroll. A few days of brow-furrowing and hand-wringing about bullying and respectful conduct followed in the press, and a few days of David Brent jokes followed on Twitter. Then Pearson apologised and the whole incident slipped away like, well, water off a duck's arse.

But it's worth remembering here, for two reasons. One, while last year's title[4] basically wrote itself — cheers Steven! — we were really struggling this time around. And two, because of the next line of the press conference, which was sort of overlooked in the fallout. Baker, quite reasonably, agrees with Pearson that he isn't flexible enough to get his head into the sand. And Pearson shoots right back:

"*I can*, you can't."

Emphasis ours. We know Ian Baker isn't an ostrich. But Nigel Pearson, by his own admission, absolutely and definitely is. And perhaps the implication that an ostrich can't hold down a proper job came back to haunt him in the end, as Pearson, at the time of writing, has just been sacked by Leicester City. Apparently they did it over the phone. Let's just hope there were no dogs nearby.

*** END OF AVIAN INTERLUDE ***

4 It's called "This Does Not Slip", which obviously you know because you bought it and you read it to your children every night, even the grown-up words, even the most grown-up word that Alan Pardew threw at Manuel Pellegrini.

MAY 2nd

Leicester 3-0 Newcastle

Aston Villa 3-2 Everton

Liverpool 2-1 QPR

Sunderland 2-1 Southampton

Swansea 2-0 Stoke

West Ham 1-0 Burnley

Manchester United 0-1 West Bromwich

MAY 3rd

Chelsea 1-0 Crystal Palace

Tottenham 0-1 Manchester City

MAY 4th

Hull 1-3 Arsenal

30th May, 2012

After Kenny Dalglish was removed from the Liverpool hotseat — his owners frustrated by his long term vision and his handling of the Luis Suarez crisis — the time was for Fenway Sports Group to try something new. Roberto Martinez looked like he would make the move from Wigan Athletic, but in the end the young man from Swansea, with an outstanding track record of getting a club promoted while playing nice football, got the job.

Rodgers impressed enough in his first season. He altered the squad, got rid of those he was not interested in, and alienated Andy Carroll. Liverpool finished seventh and there was enough about the new style, if not all of the results, to suggest that Liverpool had hired a competent coach. Yes, there was gobbledygook spoken, but that's what young managers do: they Brent.

And then, he dared to make us all dream. The nation went through a similar period of bated breath as when the Duchess of Cambridge made her way to the Lindo wing. We all waited to see if Steven Gerrard could get what he deserved, if Suarez could fire them to the title, if Rodgers could prove what he kept telling us all — that he was a journalist — and if Liverpool fans could cry with happiness in the stands. It was not to be, Suarez left, and so did Gerrard, in spirit.

Still, they went again, but this time the going was not so good. Daniel Sturridge's injuries robbed them of goals, the new signings didn't settle, and Rodgers alienated Mario Balotelli. They struggled to fifth, a slight hope of Champions League. Not good enough, thought many Liverpool fans, who appeared to tire of him overnight. Get the plane out, someone thought, let's do this. RODGERS OUT, RAFA IN.

30th May, 2015

Rafael Benitez strides down a Boston boulevard, Stevia-sweetened frappuccino in hand, walking with John Henry next to him. Released from Napoli[1], the two discuss football. Happy to work with the statistical knowledge of the Liverpool committee and backroom, Benitez outlines his approach to the game. He wants positional discipline and tactical intelligence. Matches will be won on the break with direct football — he calls it vertical — and cup competitions are there to be won with specific game plans.

It starts well in his first season. He gets the players he wants. Marek Hamsik from Napoli and, despite a little acrimony, Gareth Barry on a free from Everton. Dirk Kuyt cancels an agreement to join Feyenoord and enjoys an exceptional season at right-back, replacing the departed Glen Johnson. Liverpool finish in the Champions League positions, though Philippe Coutinho is alienated.

In his second season, it all falls apart. FSG refuse to back him in the transfer market with as much money as he requires, and James Milner fails to arrive after a miserable season at Arsenal[2]. Benitez gets to the Champions League quarter-finals, where they beat Real Madrid 1-0 at home but lose to a 3-1 defeat in the return leg. Despite being in third, the defeat knocks their confidence, and the fans turn on him when they play Arsenal with a midfield of Thiago Motta, Lucas, Joe Allen, Cheick Tiote and Javi Moreno, behind Edinson Cavani running the channels. They lose 2-0. Get the plane out, someone thinks. BENITEZ OUT, KENNY AND STEVEN IN.

30th May, 2017

John Henry is spotted with Steven Gerrard in LA (mint tea) with Kenny Dalglish (Robinson's orange barley water) then following up with a meeting two days later in Boston. The agreement is made that Dalglish will co-manage with Gerrard as he learns the ropes of management. Gerrard insists that he will continue to play football where required, having kept himself fit with MLS. He installs himself

1 You'll forgive us for not predicting that he'd get the Madrid job. You'll forgive us for not really believing it even now.

2 We probably should have got this one right, though, since James Milner comes out in hives if he tries to live anywhere south of Birmingham.

as club captain and plays every minute of every match. Dalglish is given the brunt of the criticism by the fans as they win 12 points in three months, half of whom believe that the club need to build around Gerrard in midfield. A convoy of planes flies over Anfield: first DALGLISH OUT (WE DO LOVE YOU, then THOUGH KENNY), STEVEN TO, and finally STAY AND BE MANAGER.

30th October, 2017

Gerrard reluctantly agrees to retire after discussions with Henry and his coaching team (camomile infusions all round), who point out he ran an average of just 2.4km per game while still topping the charts for number of shots in the Premier League, personally outshooting both Manchester City and Spurs combined. The rest of the season peters out as Gerrard is unable to reinvigorate an ageing squad, and he fails to impress the fans enough to keep himself in a job for another year. Liverpool finish eighth, and Gerrard agrees to come out of retirement and start playing again in MLS. A plane flies over Anfield: GERRARD OUT, DIRK (AND KOLO) IN

MAY 9th

Everton 0-2 Sunderland
Aston Villa 1-0 West Ham
Hull 0-1 Burnley
Leicester 2-0 Southampton
Newcastle 1-1 West Bromwich
Stoke 3-0 Tottenham
Crystal Palace 1-2 Manchester United

MAY 10th

Manchester City 6-0 QPR
Chelsea 1-1 Liverpool

MAY 11th

Arsenal 0-1 Swansea

Jose Mourinho grimaced. All around him, Liverpool fans were dancing. Red flags were waving, voices were raised in song. "And now you're gonna believe us, and now you're gonna believe us, and now you're gonna believe us ... We're gonna win the league."

Brendan Rodgers bounded towards him, a huge grin smeared over the bottom half of his face. Jose looked quickly for an exit, but too late: Rodgers was on him, shaking his hand, squeezing his elbow. "Hard luck, Jose. Hard luck. Though your boys were outstanding today. Outstanding. But we've put together something special here ..."

Jose smiled weakly and managed to pull his hand away. He felt the bile rise in his throat. His phone buzzed; he didn't need to check, he knew it would be Rafa. He glanced back out to the pitch. Steven Gerrard was standing in the centre circle, basking in the adulation of his giddy fans. "We go to Crystal Palace!" As Jose looked, Liverpool's captain began to grow. Seven feet, eight feet, ten, twelve ... soon Gerrard stood fifty feet tall in the middle of the Anfield pitch. His head blocked out the sun.

Liverpool's captain bent down and reached for Jose, easily snatching him with his giant thumb and forefinger. He pulled Jose into the air; Jose kicked and squirmed, but he couldn't escape. A sea of Liverpool fans looked up at him, laughing and pointing and taking photographs as he thrashed uselessly. Gerrard's mouth opened wide and he raised Jose above his head, above his massive teeth, above his giant, muculent[1], quivering tongue. He let go. Jose fell ...

... and Jose Mourinho woke up.

It was Sunday morning. It was just a dream; it had been just a dream every night for the last two years. He wasn't in Liverpool; he was in Chelsea. He hadn't lost; he'd won. This year, he'd won. He was a champion. Chelsea were the finest team in the land, and Liverpool were irrelevant again.

So why couldn't he sleep?

He made his way to the stadium, his focus slowly returning. He'd given his team a few days off: partly because they'd earned it, partly because it would make any victory here that little bit funnier. For the same reason, he decided to bring in a couple of the kids. The season was over, after all, and nothing draws a sting out of an opponent's focus than the sense that while it might matter very much to them, it doesn't quite to you.

Why couldn't he sleep?

All through the game, it bugged him, even as he went through the motions on the touchline. A munificent smile at the guard of honour; a dismissive wave of the arms when Cesc Fabregas flew through Raheem Sterling; a smile and a fistpump when John Terry nutted Chelsea into the lead past a slipping Gerrard; a scowl and a tut when Liverpool's captain nicked the equaliser. Always his mind elsewhere: back in bed, back at Anfield.

Why couldn't he sleep?

After the game, the day passed in a blur. A handshake, a press conference, some platitudes, some nodding. Even the revelation that Rodgers had removed his captain ten minutes before the end of a must-win game in order to get him an ovation could only raise half a smile; so, too, Gerrard's tart dismissal of that same ovation. His dinner, delicately cooked and exquisitely flavoured, was boiled potatoes; his wine, robust and full-bodied, was vinegar.

1 Mmmm. Tasty, tasty muculent.

Sleep was coming. Sleep was not coming.

Jose Mourinho lay down in bed. He stared blankly into the darkness. Is this how great men become great, he wondered. Do they spend their lives running from the horrors that live behind their own eyelids? Before Anfield, it had been Barcelona that haunted his every sleeping moment; before that, Benfica. And before that? He didn't know. He didn't want to know.

Jose Mourinho closed his eyes, and Morpheus quickly overwhelmed him. He abandoned the facts again, and was back in Liverpool. He could hear singing. He could see dancing. There were flags.

MAY 16th

Southampton 6-1 Aston Villa
Burnley 0-0 Stoke
QPR 2-1 Newcastle
Sunderland 0-0 Leicester
Tottenham 2-0 Hull
West Ham 1-2 Everton
Liverpool 1-3 Crystal Palace

MAY 17th

Swansea 2-4 Manchester City
Manchester United 1-1 Arsenal

MAY 18th

West Bromwich 3-0 Chelsea

MAY 20th

Arsenal 0-0 Sunderland

With the top four positions now almost certainly decided, we were granted access to the summer plans of the managers of those who have qualified for Champions League football. Brendan Rodgers, obviously, is not in this group, but he insisted we included his plans to, as he told us that, 'it's not right that the world be denied my expertise and inspiration purely because the process has not been statistically matched by outcomes'. Obviously, we could not argue with a man who will now take over from Steven Gerrard as the symbolic leader of Liverpool. We forgot to update our contacts book properly so we also asked David Moyes for his Manchester United plans, too, which he surprisingly sent onto us.

Jose Mourinho

Maintain current handsome look after letting myself go so studiously in my last year at Real Madrid and my first year at Chelsea. It worked, lulling the opposition into a false sense of security, exacerbated by the presence of Mohamed Salah. Next, throw Arsenal fans into utter disarray by making a bid for Olivier Giroud and praise him as the greatest striker of his generation, forcing them to decide that actually, he wasn't that good anyway and they had needed to improve on him. Then pull out of bid, and leave them stuck with him. Possibly develop a cackle?

Manuel Pellegrini

Make sure I get the deposit back from the landlord. Speak to the bank about shutting my English bank account and reroute all my payments to my Chilean bank account. Update CV and LinkedIn account (N.B. get Yaya Toure to endorse my 'inspiration' skill). Make sure to book holiday away from Australia and America to avoid International Champions Cup. Mute 'Pep Guardiola' on my Twitter account for the next three months[1]. Organise removal men for end of the season and finally remember to pay someone to actually do the packing for me this time, you don't want to go through the Madrid debacle again. Take MCFC hoodie to the charity shop. Continue this thankless slog now that it looks like Guardiola is staying at Bayern for another year. Look at squad. Cry.

Arsene Wenger

Third place and the FA Cup final. Compared to fourth place and the FA Cup final last season, it is clear that I have cracked it yet again, and Arsenal are on course for many more years of Champions League qualification. Watching plenty of videos of games from across the world, searching for a steely central defender and commanding goalkee — Oh, look at that through ball! Who's that?

Louis van Gaal

Reading list for summer: Kant, Jung, Plato, Locke, Spinoza, Bentham, Grisham, Patterson. Take scout reports on Anderson, Hernandez and Cleverley and put them in the shredder, then into the bin, then set the bin on fire. Call up Jorge Mendes and swear loudly and imaginatively. Call up Edward Woodward and swear loudly and imaginatively. Send mixtapes to Gareth Bale and David de Gea, featuring some of the finest Dutch pop music of the last thirty years.

Brendan Rodgers

Agree date with Malcolm Gladwell to discuss authorised biography, ask PA to make sure the number he gave me was the correct one, as it doesn't seem to have enough digits in. Finalise proposal to TED about series of inspirational and analytical talks aimed at revolutionising self-actualisation and achieving outstanding technical achievements as

1 Guardiola remains in Germany at the time of writing, with Pellegrini being one of the few managers in a job because the owners can't be bothered to do something otherwise. In that way Pellegrini represents most of us at work.

a group and with individual wonderful human beings. Sit for further preliminary sketches, and check the price of marble. Ask John Henry again if he still wants advice on how to manage the Boston Globe. Make sure Steven Gerrard definitely gets on the plane.

David Moyes

Why was I wasting my time in England? This is brilliant. Plan: do more of this. Unless the mighty West Ham come calling.[2]

2 They didn't. You have to wonder why someone would leave the Basque country to come back to England, but then you remember that football has utterly lost its senses. Remember the banners.

MAY 24th

Arsenal 4-1 West Bromwich
Aston Villa 0-1 Burnley
Chelsea 3-1 Sunderland
Crystal Palace 1-0 Swansea
Everton 0-1 Tottenham
Hull 0-0 Manchester United
Leicester 5-1 QPR
Manchester City 2-0 Southampton
Newcastle 2-0 West Ham
Stoke 6-1 Liverpool

Perhaps we were spoiled by last season[1], but even by the standards of the rubbish endings that life tends to offer up, this edition of the Premier League really has dribbled, slouched and heaved its way to the end. Like an old dog, too tired even to dream of chasing sticks any more, this season has being lying on the floor and farting for a while, and once the cup finals are done it will be time for one last trip to the vet.[2]

Still, credit to the players and the managers: they may have made this season largely unwatchable, but when it came to the final day, a few of them put their hands up and said "Yes, we may have made this season largely unwatchable, but when it comes to the final day, we're able to put our hands up and say 'Yes, we may have made this season largely unwatchable, but when it comes to the final day, have some goals'".

Not in the important games, obviously. Despite Victor Valdes' endearing turn as a slightly fuzzier Fabien Barthez, and despite Marouane Fellaini's rather less engaging moment of stampy stupidity[3], Hull City were unable to muster anything within the laws of the game, and so we all had to spend two hours watching Steve Bruce

---

1 Thank you Steven. Gone, but never, ever, ever, ever, ever forgotten.

2 All the best books contradict the introduction in the final chapter.

3 Not only did Fellaini stand on Paul McShane's thigh, he then managed to elbow him in the head on the way down. He may not be a footballer to everybody's taste, but you have to admire his efficiency.

drift slowly from 'quite sad' through 'very sad' and off into hitherto uncharted waters of misery.

The Premier League won't miss Hull much, for they were dreadful, but it's a shame to lose Steve Bruce's face, which consistently ranks among the top five managerial coupons for its range of expression and its surprising vulnerability. Farewell to that bountiful smile. Goodbye to those wet, gentle eyes. And adieu to that surprisingly soft voice.

Meanwhile, up on Tyneside, Newcastle contrived to miss a 4-on-0 break. Had they managed to relegate themselves while doing so, then this season might have gone down as an all-time classic; they didn't, so it won't.

Elsewhere, though, fun was breaking out. Arsenal were doing that thing they do when the pressure's off and the sun is out. Goals from all angles, smiles, ambitious and attractive football ... if only this were a more Corinthian world, where league tables were mere curiosities[4] and the game was the thing. Still, it may have come too late for the title race, and a week too early for Wembley, but an online poll later installed Jack Wilshere's goal as the next president of Burundi. Definitely a trophy. Somebody hack the top off a bus.

Charlie Austin, Danny Ings and Harry Kane all signed off their breakthrough Premier League campaigns with goals, and next season's Sophomore Slump Stakes is already shaping up to be a classic. We're predicting Kane from Ings by a nose.

Esteban Cambiasso also netted, and goes down in history as the only Premier League player in history not to do anything disappointing or upsetting over the course of a season. We think. Over the three games everybody watched Leicester, anyway.

We must end, of course, with Stoke, and with Liverpool, and with Steven Gerrard's six-gun salute. There are shellackings and there are shellackings, and this one came against a side whose previous biggest win of the season had been a 4-1 stroll in the FA Cup. Against Rochdale.

Whether individual results can and should tip the balance on managerial futures is a larger debate than we have room for here, and if performances can merit sackings on their own right than there are several players who should also be dreading their own

4 Sorry, Arsenal fans.

performance reviews.[5] Raheem Sterling was dropped for being less focused than the rest of them. He must have been clinically dead.

If he does go, though, then what a triumph. As we know from all those profiles he carefully wrote for the newspapers, Brendan Rodgers has profound and unvarying faith in his own alchemical powers. Lead into gold, Liverpool into title-winners, Emre Can into a defender. And yesterday he managed something that outstripped each of his previous achievements: he managed to transmute an end-of-season amble against Stoke into a game that might, just might, actually mean something.

In conclusion, this year's Premier League wasn't a classic. It wasn't even nearly a classic. But it has shown the truth in the old proverb: when life gives you a really massive pile of lemons, the only thing to do is to eat those lemons once or twice a week over the course of eight months, think about the lemons every second you're not eating them, talk loudly about the lemons with other lemon-eaters, and whatever else happens press on with your lemons even though the acid is burning your throat, the pith is catching in your teeth and the juice is staining your shirt.

We're nearly done now. Clean yourself up a bit. Just one more lemon to go. Or two if you're into big European lemons. The ones in the jar at the back of the cupboard. You bought them on holiday. Nobody remembers why.

5 And yet Brendan remains, using his powers of surl to evade blame, and his powers of bullshit to bullshit. While it would be deeply amusing to see the deliberately-bespectacled Jurgen Klopp have his own Anfield-inspired breakdown, it'll be far lovelier to see Brendan, cut off from his own coaches, redefine English for at least another season at Liverpool. Apparently, when he's talking to the press after a defeat, he deliberately talks too quietly for the journalists to be able to hear them, which is very funny.

FA CUP FINAL
MAY 30th, LONDON

Arsenal 4-0 Aston Villa[6]

6 It is impossible to care about this result, but Jack Wilshere being banned for leading a call-and-response chant in the parade for the FA Cup, saying Spurs were 'shit', and then the FA charging him for it, was an excellent summary of the state of the season. Pettiness over dignity.

EPILOGUE

Ideally you will be reading this in one of the many millions of copies sold, as we become football's answer to EL James. Earning a lot of money for an at best niche activity of limited interest to most people, you would imagine. More likely, you are one of six or seven people who we are lonely enough to interact with on Twitter on a regular basis.

Thank you for buying the book, the ebook, or jibbing a copy of one or the other. There's not much more to be written about the season, covered, as it was, relentlessly and hysterically by armies of newspaper and website writers, all of whom probably extracted all there was to extract before we sat down to write some footnotes on our recycled material.

Needless to say, as neither of us have a pension or any great financial security, we will be doing this again next year[7] as we try to squeeze out every penny available to us out of writing, rather than getting a valuable and valued job instead.

So, next season. It'll be the same again, yet more so. Ridiculous people, absurd decisions, terrible bigotry and ignorance, all against the background of some football actually happening. The only hope is that we all learn to improve ourselves and behave better next season. Yep, that'll happen.

7 We go again.